Tell Me What to Eat
if I Have
Headaches and
Migraines

by
Elaine Magee, M.P.H., R.D.

ROSEN
PUBLISHING
New York

This edition published in 2009 by:

The Rosen Publishing Group, Inc.
29 E. 21st Street
New York, NY 10010

First published as *Tell Me What to Eat if I Have Headaches and Migraines*
by New Page Books / Career Press. End matter copyright © 2009 by
The Rosen Publishing Group, Inc.

The information in this book does not substitute for professional,
medical diagnosis and treatment.

Design by Nelson Sá

Library of Congress Cataloging-in-Publication Data

Magee, Elaine.
Tell me what to eat if I have headaches and migraines / by Elaine
Magee.
    p. cm.—(Tell me what to eat)
Includes bibliographical references.
ISBN-13: 978-1-4042-1838-3 (library binding)
1. Headache—Diet therapy. 2. Migraine—Diet therapy. I. Title.
RC392.M245 2009
616.8'4910654—dc22

                                                                2008014943

Manufactured in the United States of America

Acknowledgments

T hankfully there are dedicated researchers in the area of headaches and migraines who have been conducting further study on the relationship between diet and headache over the recent years. Their research efforts gave me a lot to work with while writing this book, and I thank them all for making this possible. It is my hope and wish that their hard work and my reporting about it in this book will ultimately help make millions of headache sufferers more comfortable through the years to come.

I want to send a special thank-you out to a very exceptional headache expert—Dr. Frederick Freitag: You were just about the only headache expert who had the answers to my tedious diet and headache questions and took the time to answer all of them. I was beginning to think some of my questions would never be answered, and then there you suddenly were, saving the day. I am eternally grateful for your time, your answers, and your willingness to write the foreword to this book.

Many thanks also to my wonderful research assistant, Jamie Renton, who spent hours reading labels for the supermarket lists in this book.

Table of Contents

Foreword

As one of the associate directors of the Diamond Headache Clinic in Chicago, the largest private headache clinic in the United States, and a member of the board of directors of the National Headache Foundation, it is not uncommon for me to have contact with press interested in headaches and looking for something new on migraines. So when Elaine Magee contacted me and left a message with my secretary regarding information on diet and headaches, I was expecting it to be another such call. I was most pleasantly surprised to learn that the scope of the inquiry was to be more extensive and for a larger purpose: a book on diet and headaches.

The Diamond Headache Clinic has long maintained that dietary factors are important for many of our patients with migraines and other headaches. Therefore, we have developed an extensive series of recommendations on foods for headache sufferers to avoid. We have also conducted extensive research with our colleagues from the Rosalind Franklin University of Medicine and Science to examine the content of vasoactive amine in foods, especially for those who are taking a monoamine oxidase inhibitor as part of their treatment. This has led to an easing of the dietary restrictions for our patients who must take these potent medications for their preventive treatment.

But avoiding foods that contribute to headaches only constitutes one of the trigger factors for headaches. So we instruct patients in the roles other factors serve as contributors to their headaches. The use of diaries to record the linkage between these triggering factors and their headaches may serve as an empowering tool for them in their headache management.

All of this occurs in the setting of appropriate diagnosis of the headache disorder and establishment of treatment regimens that involve education, acute medications, and, in most patients, preventive medications to limit the frequency of their headaches. Additional nonpharmacologic modalities are also commonly used as part of these components of treatment.

All of which brings us to where we are now: empowering the patient. My friend, Roger Cady, M.D., of Springfield, Missouri, one of the foremost physician educators in the United States, speaks of migraine management as being "patient centered." I, coming from educational training in medicine as an osteopathic physician, learned early on and throughout my training of the need for a "holistic" approach in patient management. That term has become waylaid in our language to mean other than its original intent of being all-encompassing. So regardless of how we view these approaches to medicine, we find that the patient is at the center of it all—the patient is the controller, director, and leader of the healthcare delivery process when all is said and done. The role of the healthcare team becomes one of providing the necessary tools to empower the patient.

Elaine Magee is empowering you through this book to manage your headaches! Unlike any diet book for headaches I've ever seen, this book begins at the beginning. That is, it begins with a diagnosis of headache disorders from which the reader can develop an understanding of how a variety of factors—medical, behavioral, and dietary—may come together to contribute to the process that results in migraines and other headache disorders. While the information here is not exhaustive, it is not meant to be. It is meant to serve as a guide to you in your self-management of your headache situation and help you to be an effective partner with your healthcare provider in understanding your illness.

One of the greatest beauties of this book is that it recognizes that you and I are only human. Although we may want to make all the positive changes espoused here while shedding the negatives all at once, that also means making a lifetime worth of changes all at the same time, which is hard to do. However, if we take it one step at a time, just like a child learning to walk, it becomes a process that is more easily mastered and more likely to be adhered to over the course of time.

If you are looking for a cookbook for a headache sufferer, this is not the book for you—although Ms. Magee does include a chapter full of tasty recipes. If you are looking for a book to help you handle migraines better by managing your diet better, then this is the book for you. I hope that through your use of this wonderful book you will become an effective manager of your headaches through your diet!

Frederick Freitag, D.O.
Associate Director, Diamond Headache Clinic

Introduction

I f you are reading this book, chances are pretty good that you suffer from painful headaches or migraines often enough that you felt you needed more information. Please know my heart goes out to you, and it is my deepest wish and prayer that you find relief.

Headaches are a highly individual disease. That means you need to find the specific foods, eating patterns, or other factors that are your personal headache triggers. Only then can you begin to prevent some of your headaches. The first few chapters of this book will give you the clues and copious lists of possible triggers based on what I found in scientific literature and reports from headache clinics and associations. Even if various experts disagreed on the validity of certain triggers, I still included them in this book. I would rather you know all the possible triggers, because if it were me, I would rather know what at least some experts have found to be triggers in their patients.

I wrote this book as if I were suffering from headaches and migraines and wanted to get my hands on all the right information—information that would help me understand and, more importantly, relieve me of at least some of my headaches. Fortunately I don't have chronic migraines, but I know plenty of close friends who do, and I have watched them suffer over the years. It is my hope that as you read this book, you sense my compassion for you—as if I were holding your hand as you walk through this book.

I only had a migraine-type headache once. I found myself having pretty bad allergies while vacationing in Hawaii for the first time, but didn't take any medication for it while I was there. I kept thinking to myself: Allergies? What am I allergic to here—suntan lotion? But I was most definitely allergic to the plant life, and when the plane took off to take me back to the mainland, my first migraine-type headache was born. I took the one generic aspirin that was hiding in the bottom of my purse, but that didn't even touch it. I found myself crying on and off during the five-hour flight due to the relentless pain and throbbing. And it was in that dark, lonely place that I realized this may be what my various friends experience when they have their migraine headaches—and my heart went out to them, and my heart goes out to you, too. So while I don't officially "know your pain," I got a taste of it that fateful plane trip home from Maui.

In Chapter 1, we will go through some general medical questions and answers regarding headaches and migraines. Don't miss the list of various headache associations and clinics where you can get more information or help, or perhaps even become a member. Chapter 2 goes through the different types of headaches (the more common ones), while Chapter 3 answers questions about the relationship between diet and headaches that you may be wondering about. You'll find the 10 Food Steps to Freedom in Chapter 4, and recipes to help your headaches in Chapter 5 (these recipes are healthful alternatives to foods that have been identified as headache triggers). Chapter 6 helps you with your supermarket shopping by offering lists of foods to avoid (those containing MSG, aspartame, and nitrates/nitrites), as well as lists of some healthy choices and alternatives to those headache triggers. And lastly, given everything presented in this book as possible triggers, you will find a list of restaurant do's and don'ts in Chapter 7.

I hope the information in this book serves you well, and I wish you all the best of health as well as relief from your headaches.

Elaine Magee

 Chapter 1

The Who, What, Where, Why, and How of Headaches and Migraines

W elcome to the medical chapter of this book. My aim is to answer some of your general questions about headaches and migraines first, before we get into the nitty-gritty of the food and diet aspect (that starts in Chapter 3). I have tried to think of all the possible questions you may have, and I hope we've answered questions you didn't even know you had.

 How many people suffer from headaches and migraines?

More than 45 million Americans seek medical attention for severe or chronic headaches. Within this group is the subgroup of people who specifically suffer from migraine headaches, which is around 16 to 18 million people. Another source estimates that 23 million adults in the United States suffer from them.

 How do doctors diagnose headaches?

If you have headache symptoms, the first important step is to make an appointment with your doctor. He or she will probably perform a physical examination and headache evaluation where you will describe your headache history and characteristics of your headaches.

Certain tests may be performed so the doctor can get as much information as possible, including a CAT (computerized axial tomography) scan or MRI (magnetic resonance imaging). These tests will take cross-section pictures of your brain, and can reveal any abnormal areas or problems.

If you have lost consciousness during your headaches, an EEG (electroencephalogram) may be performed as well.

If your headache symptoms seem to get worse or occur more often, you may want to consider asking your doctor for a referral to a headache specialist or headache clinic.

How are headaches often treated?

A treatment plan for your headaches depends on all sorts of things, including the type of headache you are having, how often you have them, and the suspected cause of your particular headache. The treatment should be designed to meet your specific needs, and it may involve a combination of counseling on diet and lifestyle changes, medications (to prevent or treat your headaches when they occur), stress management, biofeedback, hypnosis, and so on.

What causes the pain we feel during a migraine or headache?

General headache pain is thought to result from signals between the brain and the blood vessels and the nerves around them. When a headache is taking place, specific nerves of the blood vessels and head muscles are "activated," and they send pain signals to the brain. Researchers are still trying to understand why these signals get activated to begin with.

Migraine headache pain is related to a "pain center" in the midbrain area. Researchers suspect that a migraine begins when hyperactive nerve cells send out impulses to the blood vessels, causing constriction at first. Then a dilation (or expansion) of these blood vessels results, along with the release of prostaglandins, serotonin, and other inflammatory substances that encourage the pulsing to be painful.

What are migraines?

Migraine headache pain is intense and throbbing, and usually occurs on one side of the head. It is often accompanied by nausea, vomiting, and sensitivity to light or noise. Migraines, thought to be the most debilitating type of headache, are now considered to be a neurological disease with a hereditary link.

Are migraines hereditary?

There is a family history of migraines in about 90 percent of migraine sufferers, so the answer is yes. Sometimes people don't think they have a family history of migraines because members may have thought they had sinus or tension-type headaches, when in actuality they were having migraines.

It is estimated that when both parents have a history of migraines, there is a 70 percent chance that the child will also develop them.

If only one parent has a history of migraines, the risk drops to 25 to 50 percent.

What physiological changes occur before or during a migraine?

Stress is one of the most common triggers of migraines, so let's take a closer look at what is happening in the brain during stress that causes them. During a stressful event, your body reacts much like it would to an event where you need to physically get yourself quickly out of harm's way (known as the "fight or flight" response). When this happens, certain chemicals in the brain are released to help the body combat the situation. These released chemicals can provoke the vascular changes that bring on a migraine. The severity of the migraine can actually increase due to repressed emotions and fatigue surrounding the stress (anxiety, worry, and excitement can increase muscle tension and dilate blood vessels further).

We know that blood vessels dilate (expand) as a result of a migraine headache. Can decreasing this dilation of the blood vessels bring faster relief?

One of the latest theories on what actually causes migraines in the body involves trigeminal nerve activation in the brain, causing a drop in the level of serotonin (a brain chemical that affects pain receptors), which may cause blood vessel changes.

How long do migraines last?

Migraine attacks can last from four hours to three days, and often leave a person unable to work or do their regular daily activities.

What is a migraine "aura"?

Migraines with auras happen in about 20 to 30 percent of migraine sufferers. An aura generally includes visual symptoms such as:

- Bright flashing dots or lights.
- Distorted vision.
- Temporary vision loss.
- Wavy or jagged lines.

An aura generally presents itself one hour before a migraine attack and lasts from 15 to 60 minutes. The symptoms always last less than one hour.

Auras have also been reported to include nonvisual symptoms, such as ringing in the ears or a change in smell, taste, or touch.

 What types of medications are available to treat migraines?

Work with your doctor or neurologist to figure out what, if any, of the following medications may be appropriate for you:

- **Pain-relief medications.** Over-the-counter pain-relief medications are effective for some people with migraines, and include active ingredients such as ibuprofen, aspirin, acetaminophen, and caffeine. Be cautious when taking these: they can sometimes contribute to a headache, or overuse can cause a dependency problem and "rebound" headaches. See your doctor if you are taking these medications more than three times a week (there may be prescription medications much more effective for you).

- **Antinausea medications.** These medications may be prescribed by your doctor to relieve the nausea that can accompany migraines.

- **Abortive medications.** These are medications that are taken at the first sign of a migraine and are designed to help stop the process that causes the headache pain. They work by constricting the blood vessels, attempting to bring them back to normal, and therefore relieve the throbbing pain.

- **Preventive or prophylactic medications.** These may be prescribed if your headaches are severe and frequent. These medications are generally taken on a daily basis, with the intention of reducing the frequency and severity of the headaches.

> **NOTE:**
>
> All of these treatments should be used under the direction of a headache specialist or doctor familiar with migraine treatments. As with any medication, it is important to follow the instructions on the label or given to you by your doctor.

 What medications are best for menstrual migraines?

There is really only one type of medication used to treat menstrual migraines—non-steroidal anti-inflammatory drugs (NSAIDs). The ones most often used for menstrual migraines are:

- Orudis.
- Advil.
- Motrin.
- Nalfon.
- Naprosyn.
- Relafen.

The general rule of thumb is to start taking the dose recommended by your doctor two to three days before your menstrual period starts, and to continue taking them until your period ends. Gastrointestinal side effects are small because women generally take this type of medication for only a short period of time each month.

If you are taking birth control pills, speak to your doctor directly, but many recommend taking a NSAID starting on the 19th day of a cycle, and ending on the second day of the next cycle.

What are the options for migraines when you are pregnant?

This can be tough because no treatment is recommended to treat migraines during pregnancy. Medications can affect the uterus and cross the placenta, affecting the baby.

Speak to your obstetrician before taking any medication while pregnant.

What are the most common migraine triggers?

Stress is the No. 1 migraine trigger, and, according to some estimates, certain foods and beverages may be responsible for triggering up to 30 percent of migraines.

Migraines can be triggered by many factors, including:

- Stress. (Emotional stress is one of the most common triggers of a migraine.)
- Anxiety.
- Bright light or reflective sunlight.
- Smoking and second-hand smoke. (Nicotine stimulates blood vessels in the brain to constrict or narrow. Smoking also stimulates the nerves in the back of the throat, which contributes to headache pain.)
- Any change in sleeping habits (either getting too much or too little sleep).
- Menstrual cycle and hormonal changes in women.
- Changes in weather, climate, or barometric pressure.
- Changes in altitude or time zones.
- Fasting or skipping meals.
- Specific foods.
- Excessive caffeine consumption or caffeine withdrawal.

What are some other possible migraine triggers?

- Depression, anxiety, or strong emotions.
- Physical exercise.
- Alcohol (red wine and port).
- Aspartame (an artificial sweetener found in diet sodas, light yogurts, and other sugar-free or light food products).
- MSG (an additive found in many packaged food products and Chinese/Asian cuisine).
- Nitrates/nitrites (an additive found in cured meats, including hot dogs, sausage, bacon, and cold cuts).
- Tyramine (an amino acid found in aged cheese, yeast, and pickled or marinated foods).

F.Y.I. **What Does Exercise Have to Do With Headaches?**

Here's what's going on when you exercise or exert yourself: the muscles of the head, neck, and scalp need more blood to circulate, causing the blood vessels to swell, which can lead to headaches caused by physical exertion.

- Certain foods, including chocolate and citrus fruits.
- Birth control pills or hormone therapy.
- Certain medications that dilate blood vessels.
- Overuse of pain medications (may trigger rebound headaches).
- Polluted air.
- Odors from things such as perfume, paint, dust, and certain flowers

 Are certain medical conditions associated with migraines, and are there potential intertwined problems that should be considered?[1]

The following are medical conditions that are more commonly associated with migraines:

- Asthma.
- Chronic fatigue syndrome.
- Hypertension.
- Raynaud's phenomena (occurs when blood vessels narrow, causing pain and discoloration, usually in the fingers).
- Stroke.
- Sleep disorders.

The following are potential intertwined problems that should be considered when treating women with migraines:

- Eating disorders.
- Irritable bowel syndrome.
- Mood disorders.
- PMS and premenstrual dysmorphic disorder.

F.Y.I. For Women Only

- Migraine headaches are three times more common in women than men.
- An estimated 20 percent of all American women say they've experienced a migraine at some point in their lives.
- Nearly half of all women who visit their doctors for migraine treatment report a greater vulnerability to attacks during menstruation.
- Nearly 75 percent of the people who suffer from migraines are of the female persuasion.

Any of the hormonal phases women go through (monthly and throughout their lives) can change their risk of migraines. I call these hormonal phases the "3 Ms": menarche, menstruation, and menopause. Some experts think it's the changes in estrogen levels during these times that help trigger headaches.

Other hormonal phases include:

Pregnancy: Migraines often get worse after the first trimester of pregnancy, but often improve after the birth of the baby.

Perimenopause: When women's ovaries begin to turn off, migraines can get worse. Some researchers note that HRT (hormone replacement therapy) can help prevent migraines, with the estrogen patch helping the most because it releases a more constant flow of estrogen.

Menopause and beyond: Headaches often get better during this time in a woman's life.

⇨

The Menstruation Connection

A recent study indicated that women who suffer from migraines are more likely to have an attack during the premenstrual time (two days before menstrual bleeding) through the first three days of their period. These migraines also tend to be more severe than the migraines that women have during other times of the month.[2]

A Pill in Time Saves Nine

Neurologist Stephen Silberstein, M.D., F.A.C.P., of the Headache Clinic at Thomas Jefferson University Medical College in Philadelphia discovered in a recent study that women can help prevent menstrual headaches by taking migraine-preventive drug therapy two days before menstruation typically begins, and continuing it for the next four days. Of the women taking two pills a day (a 2.5 milligram dose each) of Frova (a medication usually used to relieve migraine pain and symptoms once one has begun), 41 percent experienced menstrual migraines. Compare this to the 67 percent who had migraines while taking the placebo. (This medication is not advised for women with heart disease or uncontrolled high blood pressure.)[3]

 Are there any herbal or vitamin supplements that may help prevent migraines?

Herbal or vitamin supplements that may help prevent migraines include:

1. Feverfew.

They may have had it right back in the first century when a famous Greek botanist noted the herb feverfew as being a valuable headache remedy. Hundreds of years later, researchers are still studying its effects.

Feverfew has been shown to be useful for migraine prevention in about 40 percent of patients, according to Dr. Christina Peterson, M.D., medical director of the Oregon Headache Clinic. Keep in mind, though, that it may take two months of use to be most effective.

If you have milder migraines (which sounds like a contradiction in terms, I know), studies in Europe suggest that you may help prevent migraines with a daily supplementation of 125 milligrams of dried feverfew leaf extract. This may work by preventing large and fast reductions in serotonin levels. (If you are allergic to ragweed—a botanical cousin to feverfew—or if you have compromised kidney function, this is not for you.)

2. Riboflavin.

Although preliminary, some new research has found that 400 milligrams a day of riboflavin (a.k.a. vitamin B-2) over the course of three months results in fewer than half the migraines than one would normally suffer. (The daily value for riboflavin is just 2 milligrams.) The average number of headaches per patient decreased from four per month (before the study) to two per month (during treatment with riboflavin). But that's not all! The research also found that the migraines also tended to be less severe and of shorter duration compared to the ones experienced by those taking the placebo. Researchers suspect it may have something to do with riboflavin influencing glucose metabolism in the brain.[4]

Hang in there if you try this, because you need to take it for three months before you can tell if it is helping you. Also, a few adverse reactions were reported during the study, including diarrhea, abdominal pain, and facial redness.

 Are there other alternative therapies I should consider?

This isn't a book about alternative therapies and headaches, but I wanted to at least point you in the right direction should you want to consider any of these alternative therapies. (You can try these even if you want to continue with your medications.)

Other alternative therapies include:

- An ice pack placed on the painful area of your head, such as the temples, back of the neck, or forehead.

- Take a warm bath or shower, take a nap, or take a walk.

- Apply gentle, steady rotating pressure to the painful area of your head with your index finger and/or thumb. Maintain this pressure for seven to 15 seconds, then release and repeat.

- If you happen to have excessive muscle contractions in your neck, physical therapy exercises that you can do every day are often helpful. Your doctor may be able to refer you to a physical therapist for a consultation.

- Try acupuncture. The Consensus Statement on Acupuncture by the National Institutes of Health (1997) states that for conditions including headaches, lower back pain, menstrual cramps, and carpal tunnel syndrome, acupuncture was useful as an additional treatment or as an acceptable alternative to be included in a comprehensive pain-management program.

Can biofeedback help migraines?

Biofeedback can be very helpful for migraine sufferers for which stress is one of their headache triggers. It helps people to recognize the stressful situations that trigger migraines as well as teaches them techniques that will reduce the stress in their bodies. Biofeedback involves attaching small metal sensors (electrodes) to the skin that measure the amount of muscle tension or skin temperature.

These electrodes give you instant feedback on what techniques are working to help you reduce stress and open up blood flow to these areas of your body. If your migraine begins slowly, some people can use biofeedback to stop the attack before it is fully underway.

Can massage help migraines?

Massage is a great way to reduce stress and relieve muscle tension, which goes without saying. Peppermint and lavender oils, when used to massage the skin, may help manage migraines as well. It can't hurt to try this one! The worst that can happen is your skin is softer and your stress level goes down a few pegs. Ask someone to rub your neck and back, or treat yourself to a massage when you feel your stress building and muscles tensing.

What is the common treatment for headaches in general?

Traditional therapies seem to rely heavily on prescription medications. But more and more headache clinics and headache experts are taking a holistic approach to headache management, including diet therapy.

In general though, if you have occasional severe headaches, over-the-counter pain-relief medications can usually treat them effectively. However, if you have frequent mild headaches that occur more than three or four times a week, you could wind up taking too many over-the-counter analgesics, which is not a good thing. When you use these too frequently, you can actually promote chronic daily headaches (known as rebound headaches). It's a very good idea to see a physician about your frequent headaches, even if they are mild.

Can Botox help prevent headaches?

Botox may be considered the fountain of youth by celebrities and countless others, but can it help headaches? A few studies over the past couple of years have indicated that Botox helps migraine sufferers, although the most effective places on the head to inject the Botox is still unclear. A recent German study specifically looked at the success of Botox for the treatment of migraines, using different injection sites (various muscle groups in the forehead and/or neck). They found no significant reduction of migraine frequency, number of days with migraine, or amount of drugs needed to treat the migraine in those using Botox therapy compared to those in the placebo group. The researchers do note that other injection sites and other doses of Botox might be effective in a defined subgroup of patients.[5]

When should a headache be considered an emergency situation?

Is it the first headache you've ever had? If so, treat it as an emergency.

Is it the worst headache you've ever had? If so, treat it as an emergency.

You could find yourself in a life-or-death situation if you are having an aneurysm (when a blood vessel opens and blood floods into the brain). Some types of headache are signals of more serious, potentially life-threatening disorders that require immediate medical attention. These types include:

- Sudden, severe headache.
- Sudden, severe headache associated with a stiff neck.
- Headache associated with fever.
- Headache associated with convulsions.
- Headache accompanied by confusion or loss of consciousness.
- Headache following a blow to the head.
- Headache associated with pain in the eye or ear.

- Persistent headache in a person who was previously headache-free.
- Recurring headache in children.
- Headache that interferes with normal life.

 Where else can you go for help if you suffer from headaches and migraines?

Here are some resources and organizations available to everyone:

American Academy of Neurology

Telephone: 1-800-879-1960

Web site: www.aan.com

Description: A membership organization representing neurologists worldwide. Located in Saint Paul, Minnesota.

American Council for Headache Education

Telephone: 1-856-423-0258

Web site: www.achenet.org

Description: Provides a quarterly newsletter and various other resources. Located in Mount Royal, New Jersey.

The Cleveland Clinic Headache Center

Telephone: 1-800-223-2273

Web site: www.ccf.org

Description: Provides a listing of doctors and their specialties. Located in Cleveland, Ohio.

Diamond Headache Clinic, LTD

Telephone: 1-800-432-3224

Web site: www.diamondheadache.com

Description: Clinic for those suffering from headaches and migraines. Located in Chicago, Illinois.

Excedrin Headache Resource Center (Bristol-Myers Squibb Co.)

Telephone: 1-800-580-4455

Web site: www.excedrin.com

Description: Provides information for those suffering from headaches, including a library of articles. Located in Wilton, Connecticut.

International Headache Society (IHS)

Telephone: +44 1625 828663

Web site: www.i-h-s.org

Description: Membership includes subscription to Cephalalgia, an international headache journal. Located in Prestbury, Cheshire, United Kingdom.

M.A.G.N.U.M. (Migraine Awareness Group: A National Understanding for Migraineurs)

Telephone: 1-703-739-9384

Web site: www.migraines.org

Description: Provides free membership, educational materials, and advocacy actions. Located in Alexandria, Virginia.

Migraine Action Association

Telephone: 01536 461333

Web site: www.migraine.org.uk

Description: Provides a telephone hotline, quarterly newsletter, and numerous leaflets on all aspects of migraines. Located in Great Oakley, Northants, United Kingdom.

Migraine Relief Center (GlaxoSmithKline)

Telephone: 1-888-825-5249

Web site: www.migrainehelp.com

Description: Provides links to various resources, product information, and other medical information.

National Headache Foundation

Telephone: 1-888-NHF-5552

Web site: www.headaches.org

Description: Provides lists of physicians who treat headaches, a bimonthly newsletter, educational materials about and treatment for headaches, as well as lists of support groups. Located in Chicago, Illinois.

National Institute of Neurological Disorders and Stroke

Telephone: 1-800-352-9424

Web site: www.ninds.nih.gov

Description: Provides brochures on headache and chronic pain. Located in Bethesda, Maryland.

World Headache Alliance

Telephone: +1 905 257 6229

Web site: www.w-h-a.org

Description: Posts top news stories related to headaches on their Web site. Located in Ontario, Canada.

The following are alternative therapy resources to look into:

Association for Applied Psychophysiology and Biofeedback

Telephone: 1-800-477-8892

Web site: www.aapb.org

Description: This is a membership organization for psychologists, nurses, physical therapists, and biofeedback and neurofeedback clinicians that serves to implement and improve biofeedback and other mind–body techniques to aid in the treatment of a variety of conditions, including headaches. Located in Wheat Ridge, Colorado.

Mind/Body Medical Institute

Telephone: 1-866-509-0732

Web site: www.mbmi.org

Description: Provides lists of participating health and wellness centers across the United States that offer relaxation training. Relaxation tapes are also sold on their Website. Located in Chestnut Hill, Massachusetts.

 What do all these words mean?

- **Abortive medications:** Medications used to stop the headache process and prevent symptoms of migraines, including pain, nausea, and sound and light sensitivity. They are most effective when used at the first sign of a migraine to stop the process.

- **Acute headaches:** Headaches that occur suddenly for the first time, with symptoms that subside after a relatively short period of time. They are usually due to an illness, infection, cold, or fever.

- **Analgesic:** Pain-relieving medication.

- **Aneurysm:** A weak part of an artery that may bulge outward and occasionally rupture and bleed. This leads to a condition called a subarachnoid hemorrhage, which produces a severe headache and stiff neck, and can sometimes be fatal.

- **Anti-inflammatory medications:** A type of medication used to decrease inflammation. This type of medication is most commonly used to treat the inflammation of arthritis and other inflammatory disorders, but can also be useful in reducing the pain of certain types of headaches.

- **Aspartame:** An artificial sweetener that may cause headaches in a small amount of sensitive people.

- **Aura:** A warning sign that a migraine is about to begin. An aura usually occurs about 10 to 30 minutes before the onset of a migraine, although it can occur as early as the night before the onset. The most common auras include blurred or distorted vision; blind spots; or brightly colored, flashing, or moving lights or lines.

- **Biofeedback:** A method used to help a person learn stress-reduction skills by providing information about muscle tension, heart rate, and other vital signs as the person attempts to relax.

- **Caffeine:** A stimulating ingredient found in coffee, tea, chocolate, and cola beverages. Caffeine is also a common ingredient in medications used to relieve headaches.

- **CAT scan (computerized axial tomography):** A diagnostic test in which X-rays and computers are used to produce an image of a cross-section of the body.

- **Chronic headaches:** Chronic headaches occur at least every other day or 15 days per month for at least six months.

- **Decongestant medications:** Medications that can be used to relieve headaches associated with sinus infections. Decongestants help relieve headache symptoms because they constrict blood vessels that cause headache pain. However, decongestants should only be used as directed, as they can be habit-forming.

- **EEG (electroencephalogram):** A test in which the electrical signals of the brain are recorded. Electrical activity detected by electrodes, or sensors, placed on a person's scalp are transmitted to a machine that records the activity.

- **Episodic:** Occurrences that come and go with or without a regular pattern.

- **Hormone headaches:** A headache syndrome common in women. They are often associated with changing estrogen levels that occur during menstruation, pregnancy, and menopause.

- **MAO inhibitors:** A class of drugs used to treat depression that may also help treat headaches. People taking MAO inhibitors should avoid eating foods containing tyramine because it can cause increased blood pressure.

- **Migraine:** A genetic neurological brain disease associated with multiple symptoms, such as severe hemispherical head pain (half head), nausea, vomiting, and sensitivity to light and noise. This very complicated brain disorder can also include other common symptoms that vary by individuals, including slurred speech, staggered walking, stroke-like symptoms, numbness and tingling on one side of the body, and diarrhea. Many people with migraines may go through their lives without head pain, but will have some of the other symptoms of migraines, such as the visual symptoms or gut-related symptoms.

- **MRI (magnetic resonance imaging):** A diagnostic test that produces very clear images of the human body without the use of X-rays. An MRI may be recommended if you are getting daily or almost daily headaches. It may also be recommended if a CAT scan does not show definitive results. An MRI is used to evaluate certain parts of the brain that are not as easily viewed with CAT scans, such as the spine at the level of the neck and the back portion of the brain.

- **MSG (monosodium glutamate):** A food additive commonly found in Chinese/Asian cuisine and some packaged food products. It may cause headaches in some sensitive people.

- **Neurologist:** A medical specialist with advanced training in the diagnosis and treatment of diseases of the brain, spinal cord, nerves, and muscles.

- **Nitrates/nitrites:** Food additives that may trigger headaches for some sensitive people. They are commonly found in processed meats, including bacon, pepperoni, hot dogs, ham, sausage, luncheon or deli-style meats, and other cured or processed meats. Some heart medications also contain nitrates.

- **Primary headaches:** Headaches that are not the result of other medical conditions. These include migraine, tension-type, and cluster headaches.

- **Rebound headaches:** Headaches that occur from over-using medications for headache pain. Exceeding label instructions or your doctor's advice can cause people to "rebound" into another headache. This can be especially dangerous with medications that contain caffeine, an ingredient included to speed up the reaction of the other ingredients.

- **Serotonin:** A neurotransmitter hormone that is involved in communicating the message to the brain to expand (dilate) or close (constrict) the blood vessels. When these blood vessels dilate and constrict, they stimulate nerves that carry pain-producing messages in the brain, leading to headache pain, particularly the pain of migraine. Serotonin is also responsible for controlling mood, attention, sleep, and pain.

- **Sinus headaches:** Headaches associated with a deep and constant pain in the cheekbones, forehead, or bridge of the nose. The pain often occurs with other symptoms, such as nasal drainage, facial swelling, fever, or feeling of "fullness" in the ears.

- **Tension-type headaches:** The most common type of headache among adults, tension-type headaches are thought to be caused by tightened muscles in the back of the neck and scalp. They are usually triggered by some type of environmental or internal stress.

- **Transformed migraines:** Coexisting migraine and tension-type headaches. Transformed migraines are chronic, daily headaches with a vascular quality.

- **Trigger:** A factor that can set off a migraine in people who are predisposed to them. Some common triggers include emotional stress, sensitivity to specific chemicals and preservatives in food, caffeine, changing weather conditions, changes in female hormones, tension, excessive fatigue, skipped meals, or changes in normal sleep patterns.

- **Tyramine:** A substance found naturally in some foods that is formed from the breakdown of protein as food ages. Generally, the longer a high-protein food ages, the greater the tyramine content. Many aged cheeses, red wine, alcoholic beverages, and some processed meats have been reported to be high in tyramine. Eating foods with tyramine can trigger migraines in some people. People taking MAO inhibitors must be careful not to eat foods containing tyramine, as this can cause increased blood pressure.

- **Vasoconstriction:** A narrowing or closing (constriction) of a blood vessel.

- **Vasodilation:** A swelling or opening (dilation) of a blood vessel.

Chapter 2

The Most Common Types of Headaches and What You Need to Know About Them

Migraine Headaches

Migraines are vascular headaches related to changes in the size of the arteries within and outside the brain. The exact causes of migraines are not yet known, but experts know they are related to changes in the brain and genetic causes. The new way of thinking is that migraines are caused by inherited abnormalities in certain areas of the brain. Many people with migraines have inherited sensitivity to certain migraine triggers, including fatigue, bright lights, and weather changes.

Here are some of the various characteristics of migraine headaches:

- Often, but not always, the pain is on one side of the head. It can be felt in the whole head, or it can shift from one side of the head to the other.
- Often it is a pounding, throbbing pain.
- Migraine headaches are often accompanied by associated characteristics, such as nausea, loss of appetite, abdominal pain, sensitivity to bright light or loud noise, dizziness, or mood changes.

- About one-fifth of migraine headaches are preceded by neurological symptoms that last a few minutes to an hour before the pain of the headache begins. These symptoms include blurred vision, sparkling lights, and numbness in the hands or face.
- Sometimes they include an "aura," with visual symptoms such as bright flashing dots or lights, blind spots, or wavy or jagged lines.
- They can last from four hours to three days.
- They usually occur one to four times a month.

Tension-Type Headaches

Tension-type headaches (muscle contraction headaches) are the most common type of headaches among adults and teens. About 30 percent to 80 percent of American adults suffer from occasional tension-type headaches, with the majority being women. About 3 percent of American adults suffer from chronic daily tension-type headaches.

These headaches tend not to pulsate, nor are they typically felt on one side of the head. They also tend not to be as severe as migraines. Tension-type headaches are also called chronic daily headaches or chronic nonprogressive headaches.

Here are some of the various characteristics of tension-type headaches:

- Pain is mild to moderate, with constant band-like pain.
- Pain is felt in the front, top, or sides of the head.
- Pain usually begins gradually, often occurring in the middle of the day.
- Headache pain can last from 30 minutes to several days.

- People with episodic tension-type headaches often have them no more than once or twice a month, but sometimes they are more frequent than this.
- Sudden onset occurs when you wake up in the morning.
- Chronic fatigue, irritability, and disturbed concentration.
- Mild sensitivity to light or noise.
- General aching of the muscles.

Common causes of this type of headache include:

- Emotional or mental stress.
- Having problems at home or a difficult family life.
- Deadlines at school or work.
- Having a new child.
- Going on vacation (believe it or not, this can be stressful for some people).
- Starting a new job or losing a job.
- Competing in sports or other activities.
- Being a perfectionist.
- Not getting enough sleep.
- Being overscheduled or having too many demands placed on you.
- Being overweight.
- Alcohol use.
- Skipping meals.
- Changes in sleep patterns and not getting enough rest.
- Excessive medication use.
- Tension.
- Depression.
- Eyestrain and neck or back strain due to poor posture.

F.Y.I. Clues to Tell the Difference Between Having a Migraine or a Tension-Type Headache

Common triggers of both tension-type headaches and migraines include:[1]

	Migraine	Tension-Type Headache
Stress	Yes	Yes
Stress "letdown"	Yes	No
Not enough sleep	Yes	Yes
Oversleeping	Yes	No
Weather changes	Yes	Yes
Hormonal changes	Yes	No
Odors	Yes	No
Missing a meal	Yes	Yes
Certain foods	Yes	No

Additive-Induced Headaches

Symptoms can begin within 20 to 25 minutes after eating products that contain additives. Some reports state that headaches brought on by foods containing MSG can occur within an hour of eating.

Look for symptoms such as:

- Pressure in the chest.
- Tightening and pressure in the face.
- Burning sensation in the chest, neck, or shoulders.
- Facial flushing.

- Dizziness.
- Headache pain across the front or sides of the head. (Unlike more classic migraines, headaches brought on by additives are usually sensed on both sides of the head.)
- Abdominal discomfort.

Experts can't agree about MSG just yet. Some headache experts assert that MSG is one of the biggest triggers. Others look to newer research, which suggests that MSG is not a typical trigger at all. Don't let this confuse you; just use your headache diary to clue you in as to what your particular headache triggers are (see Chapter 4).

Sinus Headaches

Sinuses are air-filled spaces located in your forehead, cheekbones, and behind the bridge of your nose. The sinuses produce thin mucus that drains out the channels of the nose.

Some neurologists believe that when people think they are having sinus headaches, they are actually having migraines. Sinus headaches almost never recur, so if you notice that your sinus headaches seem to be recurring, that's your first clue that you may be having migraines instead. But diagnosing one or the other can get rather confusing because people with migraines seem to see an increase in headaches depending on humidity and other environmental conditions.

Sinus headaches are generally associated with deep and constant pain in the cheekbones, forehead, or bridge of the nose. The pain usually intensifies with sudden head movement. Sinus headaches are usually accompanied by other sinus symptoms, including nasal discharge, a feeling of fullness in the ears, fever, or facial swelling.

When sinuses become inflamed, usually because of an allergic reaction, a tumor, or an infection, the inflammation will prevent the outflow of mucus. This causes a pain similar to that of a headache.

Here are some of the various characteristics of sinus headaches:

- The pain is deep and constant, and is located around the cheekbones, forehead, or bridge of the nose.
- The pain usually intensifies when you move your head suddenly or strain yourself.
- Sinus headaches usually occur with other sinus symptoms, such as nasal discharge, a feeling of fullness in the ears, fever, and facial swelling.

How Are Sinus Headaches Treated?

Treatment is generally focused on treating the infection in the sinuses using an antibiotic. Antihistamines such as Benadryl or decongestants such as Sudafed may also be used for a short period of time to help with the symptoms. Decongestants are often used to relieve headaches associated with sinus infections because they work by constricting blood vessels that cause headache pain. However, decongestants should only be used as directed, as they can be habit-forming.

What's the Relationship Between Allergies and Headaches?

Allergies don't cause headaches per se, but the allergies can cause sinus congestion, and the congestion can lead to headache pain. Keep in mind that treating your allergies will generally not relieve your headache pain; the two must be treated individually.

Can What You Eat to Reduce Hay Fever?

New research from Germany suggests that there are a few different food components that can help or hurt a person's hay fever. According to the results of a recent study, the people who ate the most trans oleic acid (a monounsaturated fat found mainly in meat, butter, milk, and cheese) were almost three times more likely to have hay fever compared to people who ate the least trans oleic acid. Researchers don't know why this would have an affect on hay fever, but suspect that this type of fat may increase oxidative stress on the immune system.

The same German study also noted that, particularly in women, hay fever risk decreased as vitamin E consumption increased. High intakes of the fish oil EPA (eicosapentaenoic acid) also seemed to lower risk of hay fever as well.[2]

Rebound Headaches

Rebound headaches are caused by the overuse or misuse of over-the-counter pain relievers or not following your doctor's advice regarding dosage. You literally "rebound" into headache after headache. What ends up happening is that when the pain medication wears off, you may experience a withdrawal reaction, which then prompts you to take more medication. This only leads to another headache and the urge to take even more medication. Eventually, many people start suffering from chronic daily headaches, more severe pain, and more frequent headaches than ever before.

The overuse of pain relievers seems to interfere with the brain centers that regulate the flow of pain messages to the nerves, worsening headache pain.

Caffeine Only Makes It Worse

This rebound reaction is especially problematic when using medications containing caffeine (caffeine is added

to speed up the reaction of the other ingredients). The caffeine in the medications, plus the caffeine so many of you consume daily in beverages such as coffee, tea, and soft drinks, makes you even more vulnerable to developing rebound headaches.

Pain-Relief Medications May Be the Cause

Commonly used pain-relief medications that can cause rebound headaches when taken in large enough amounts include:

- Aspirin.
- Sinus-relief medications.
- Acetaminophen (Tylenol).
- Nonsteroidal anti-inflammatory medications (Aleve).
- Sedatives for sleep.
- Codeine and prescription narcotics.
- Over-the-counter headache remedies that contain caffeine (Anacin, Excedrin, and Bayer Select).
- Ergotamine preparations (Cafergot, Migergot, Ergomar, Bellergal-S, Bel-Phen-Ergot S, Phenerbel-S, Ercaf, Wigraine, and Cafatine PB).
- Butalbital combination pain-relievers (Goody's Headache Powder, Supac, and Excedrin).

Hormone Headaches

Changing hormone levels in women are often associated with headaches, namely the change in hormone levels that occurs during menstruation, menarche, pregnancy, and menopause. These headaches can also be brought about through the administration of hormones; for example, while taking birth control pills.

Cluster Headaches

Although cluster headaches are perhaps the least common of the above headaches, they are perhaps the most severe type of primary headache. The pain of the cluster headache is so intense that the sufferer cannot sit still during an attack. The pain is described as a burning or piercing pain that is throbbing or constant. It is located behind one eye or in the eye area, but not changing sides. They occur much more frequently in men than women.

They are called "cluster" headaches because they tend to present as a cluster or grouping of headache attacks, each grouping lasting from two weeks to three months. The headaches are frequent with each cluster, with possibly one to three headaches a day during a cluster period. The headaches may disappear completely for months or years before the next cluster attack.

One British study on people suffering from cluster headaches found that patients can help prevent these headaches by keeping their bedrooms cool at night and avoiding steaming hot baths during times when they are prone to experience these headaches.

Here are some of the various characteristics of cluster headaches:

- Intense one-sided pain that is described as burning or piercing and throbbing or constant.
- Pain is located behind one eye or in the eye area, but doesn't change sides.
- Pain lasts a short time (usually about 30 to 90 minutes), but on some occasions may last from 15 minutes to three hours.
- Most people get one to three headaches per day during a cluster period.
- Headaches often occur at the same time each day and may also wake up the person at the same time during the night.

Chapter 3

Everything You Ever Wanted to Ask a Dietitian About Headaches and Migraines

According to Seymour Diamond, M.D., founder of the Diamond Headache Clinic in Chicago, more than 25 percent of migraine sufferers have specific triggers, including food.

The following is everything you ever wanted to ask a dietician about regarding headaches and migraines.

Can diet really help with migraines?

Of course I want the answer to be yes because I'm writing a book about what to eat if you have headaches and migraines. And, most importantly, I really want people who suffer from headaches to have some tangible ways to discourage their headaches.

Although there isn't a huge amount of research that has been done on diet and headaches, some of the studies that have been done have been very encouraging.

Your diet can impact your headache risk in two ways:

1.   Specific foods are thought to trigger headaches.
2.   Dietary habits such as skipping meals and dehydration may also play a role.

A recent study set out to find if diet counseling and tips resulted in fewer migraine attacks in headache sufferers. Of the patients from one headache clinic, 48 received one hour or more of diet counseling by a registered dietitian, who covered dietary triggers for headaches and label-reading (among other things). These patients reported a significant reduction in the number of migraine attacks they experienced per week. At the same time, patients reported a decrease in consumption of migraine trigger foods as well.[1]

Yet while some studies have supported the importance of diet as a cause of migraines, others have challenged it. But I'm not really that surprised, because the more you learn about migraines and the potential influence your diet has on them, the more you realize how complicated their relationship really is.

It's Complicated

According to Dr. Frederick Freitag of the Diamond Headache Clinic in Chicago, a suspected food may not be a trigger 100 percent of the time.

The three main complications when it comes to trigger foods are:

1.   Often foods are triggers only when they are combined with other triggers. What other types of triggers? Try stress or hormonal changes for starters. I call this the 1 + 1 = 2 explanation. In other words:

1 trigger + 1 trigger = a headache

2.   A response to a food or beverage trigger may depend on how much of the food or beverage is consumed. You may not have a problem with a small amount of a trigger food such as cheese, for example, but you may experience problems after a particular occasion where you enjoyed a larger portion.

3.   A headache may not come about for several hours to several days after eating a trigger food. This makes it a lot more difficult to find connections between eating or drinking certain items and experiencing a migraine.

 ## Ham and Cheese Sandwich... Hold the Ham and the Cheese

John is a headache sufferer who has discovered over time that, for him, the combination of ham and cheese brings on a classic migraine. John has suffered from migraines for 15 years now and says that four to five hours after eating processed meats or certain kinds of cheese, he experiences symptoms such as vision trouble, then strong pain in one temple, followed by nausea and loss of balance.

 What items are on the "Most Wanted" list of suspected migraine food triggers?

Particular substances in food may be the cause of changes in vascular tone that bring on migraines in susceptible people. Some say there could be a possible allergic-type reaction going on, and others say that's not likely. Either

way, people with migraines might want to know what the possible offenders are so that they can eliminate them (or chart their intake and any headache response) and see if it brings them some relief.

According to a survey of patients from the Princess Margaret Migraine Clinic in England:[2]

- 28 percent reported beer would bring on headaches.
- 18.4 percent reported sensitivity to all alcoholic drinks.
- 16.5 percent reported their headaches could be precipitated by cheese or chocolate.
- 11.8 percent reported sensitivity to red wine, but not white wine.

The Top 5 Most Wanted Foods and Beverages Trigger List:

1. Don't Take My Chocolate Away!

Chocolate is listed by those who suffer from migraines as a possible trigger food. Some neurologists still believe it is a migraine trigger because it contains the amino acid tyramine.

But a study a few years ago reported that 63 women who suffered from migraines or tension-type headaches were no more likely to have a headache after consuming chocolate than they were after eating carob. The connection could be that women tend to crave chocolate during hormonal changes and stress, both of which could also be triggering a headache.

The amount of chocolate consumed could be an issue, too. See if a small but satisfying amount of chocolate (avoiding large portions) can be eaten without triggering a headache.

2. This May Hurt a Bit: Cutting Caffeine

Caffeine has consistently been shown to trigger migraines when either too much or too little is consumed. Those who are addicted to daily caffeine (from food, beverages, or caffeine-containing medications) can suffer a headache as a sign of caffeine withdrawal on a particular day when they don't get the amount of caffeine they usually consume. These rebound headaches are thought to occur in up to 50 percent of migraine sufferers.

For those addicted to caffeine, the bad news is that it may help your headache situation if you cut caffeinated beverages from your diet. The good news is that decaffeinated options abound in beverage land! You may think there is a difference in taste (some people do), but a lot of people don't notice a difference. So please try to have an open mind about decaf products. You can order decaf for most of the coffee choices at coffeehouses, and most flavored teas come in decaf, too. You can also find caffeine-free soft drinks.

For more on caffeine withdrawal headaches and how to beat your addiction to caffeine, check out Step #3 of the Food Steps to Freedom in Chapter 4.

3. Tyramine

Some headache experts doubt the importance of noting tyramine-containing foods as migraine triggers because this amino acid's connection to migraines is based on rather old research. But just in case you think a food containing tyramine may be a trigger for you, I included tyramine in my "Most Wanted" trigger list. Tyramine has the ability to reduce serotonin (the "happy hormone") levels in the brain. Some sources note that larger amounts of tyramine can be found in:

- Aged cheeses.
- Red wine.
- Alcoholic beverages such as beer.

- Some processed meats.
- Avocados.
- Overripe bananas. (Some experts say it's the peel that causes the problem and that you can eat a banana without any problems as long as you shave the outside of the banana to makes sure there is no inside peel being consumed.)
- Chocolate.
- Nuts.
- Seeds.
- Pork.
- Venison.
- Soy-based foods.

For more information on tyramine, see Step #7 of the Food Steps to Freedom in Chapter 4.

 **If You Are Taking an MAO Inhibitor**

It's particularly important to avoid all foods containing tyramine if you are taking an MAO (monoamine oxidase) inhibitor to treat your headache, because the combination can trigger severe hypertension.

---

4. Nitrates/Nitrites, MSG, and Other Possible Additives

Certain food additives, including nitrates/nitrites and MSG (monosodium glutamate), are considered by some to be common headache triggers. They may increase blood flow to the brain, causing headaches in some people. (See Chapters 4 and 6 for more on these additives and how to avoid them.)

Q In your experience, what are the food and beverage migraine triggers that seem to come up most with your patients?

(Answered by Dr. Frederick Freitag of the Diamond Headache Clinic)

I must say the single worst dietary factor is caffeine, bar none. So that means coffee and cola. Next is probably chocolate, but that is probably really not a trigger so much as a migraine warning sign known as a "premonitory event." What happens is you get a food craving for chocolate, you eat the chocolate, you get the headache, and then you attribute the headache to the chocolate when, regardless of eating it, you were going to get the headache all along. After chocolate, I would have to say cheese, especially super-aged cheddars and Italian cheeses. Then you have the processed foods containing various potential triggers.

Q Is there a connection between a fatty diet and migraines?

Yes, here is yet another reason to eat a lower-fat diet! Believe it or not, there are changes in the level of certain fats circulating in your bloodstream that coincide with the triggering of migraine headaches. And the fats you ate in a meal do end up as fats circulating in your bloodstream about three hours after mealtime. Who knew?

These are the changes in blood noted in migraine research:

- High levels of blood lipids (fats).
- High levels of free fatty acids (components of fats).
- Increased ability of platelets to cluster together, which is associated with decreased levels of serotonin (the "happy hormone") and increased prostaglandin levels.

All of the above lead to vasodilation (the expanding of the blood vessels), which is the physiological change that comes right before a migraine headache.

So what can we do?

We can start by lowering the levels of blood lipids and free fatty acids in our bloodstream. This will help to decrease platelet aggregability (ability to cluster together).

How do you do this?

Eat a lower-fat diet. A study at the Chao Family Comprehensive Cancer Center looked at the initial diets of 54 migraine headache patients. Those with the highest-fat diets tended to have more frequent headaches compared to those with lower-fat diets. The patients were then counseled to limit fat to no more than 20 grams a day. (That's the same amount of fat that's in a skinless chicken breast, 2 ounces of reduced-fat cheese, 6 ounces of low-fat yogurt, and 1/8 cup of nuts.)

Although some of the patients consumed a little bit more than 20 grams a day (the mean was about 28 grams a day), the decreased fat intake still led to significant decreases in headache frequency, intensity, duration, and medication intake.[3]

Q **Why do I tend to get migraines when I skip meals?**

Can you say "hypoglycemia"?

Sometimes it isn't what you are eating that may be causing you trouble, but rather what you aren't eating. Hypoglycemia (low blood sugar) can be a migraine trigger for some people. Some people do appear to be more susceptible to having hypoglycemia than others. I'm actually one of those people.

I figured out as a young adult that I have to avoid caffeine-laden beverages because they seem to give me the shakes and a feeling of low blood sugar (weak and dizzy). I also get this feeling of low blood sugar when I don't get a chance to eat a meal or snack. I find that higher-fiber meals and snacks seem to help me avoid that hypoglycemic feeling. A bean burrito will keep me energized for hours compared to a lower-fiber, more refined meal.

So how do you avoid having hypoglycemia?

- Eat when you are hungry, and stop when you are comfortable. Don't skip meals!

- Avoid caffeinated drinks, particularly during the times of day when you are most vulnerable to hypoglycemic reactions.

- Keep your meals and snacks balanced and high in fiber, choosing beans, whole grains, fruits, and vegetables when possible.[4]

 Phenols in red wine are thought by some to be a migraine trigger. Would other phenol-containing foods be possible triggers, too?

(Answered by Dr. Frederick Freitag of the Diamond Headache Clinic)

Phenolic substances are fairly common organic substances found in trace amounts in a wide variety of foods. Many of these substances act as antioxidants and are believed to have beneficial effects on health by reducing the likelihood of developing everything from heart disease to cancer. For example, the flavonoids in red grape juice and wine are phenolic compounds. The mechanism by which headache occurs from wine, especially red wine, is poorly understood. Yet it is doubtful that the phenols are the major player, otherwise we would be getting grape juice headaches, too!

Have you found that limiting the amount of nitrates/nitrites, MSG, and aspartame consumed has been helpful or effective in decreasing headaches and migraines?

(Answered by Dr. Frederick Freitag of the Diamond Headache Clinic)

There definitely is a cause-and-effect relationship between glutamate, the stimulating amino acid found in MSG, and aspartic acid (aspartame) and migraines, so these basic compounds will often play a role in a dose-dependent fashion. I typically advise patients to begin by eliminating all of these compounds from their diets, then cautiously add them back after their headaches are controlled. Because these substances react to produce headaches quite readily, usually within hours or less of being consumed, I have patients monitor the "dose" they are able to tolerate if they insist on eating foods that are processed or use these additives.

 Is there any relationship between lowering blood pressure through healthy diet steps and decreasing headaches or headache improvement?

(Answered by Dr. Frederick Freitag of the Diamond Headache Clinic)

Almost none. Yet a big benefit of the healthy lifestyle to control blood pressure is that this same healthy diet and lifestyle eliminates many of the factors that contribute to headaches (caffeine, excessive salt, and excessive simple sugars, for example).

 Is there anything a person can do or eat to help during a migraine?

It probably depends on what your migraine symptoms are. Many experience nausea and vomiting, so it stands to reason that eating and drinking items that are easy on the stomach and easy to digest are probably best if you are able to eat food during a migraine.

If you experience nausea or stomach upset:

- Eat small meals throughout the day instead of three large meals.
- Eat slowly.

- Avoid hard-to-digest foods.
- Consume foods that are cold or room temperature to avoid nausea from the smell of hot or warm foods.
- Rest after eating, keeping your head elevated about 12 inches above your feet.
- Drink liquids between meals instead of during, and drink at least six to eight 8-ounce glasses of water a day to prevent dehydration.
- Try to eat during the times you feel less nauseated.
- Drink small amounts of clear, sweetened liquids, such as soda or fruit juice (the exception being orange and grapefruit juice because these are too acidic and may bother your stomach). Drinks containing sugar may help calm the stomach better than other liquids.

If you experience a loss of appetite:

- Try to eat something every couple of hours if you can only eat small amounts of food at a time.
- Try chilled smoothies, "instant breakfast" mixes, or other nutritional shakes.
- Drink beverages a half hour before or after meals so they do not interfere with your appetite for food.

If you have already vomited or are extremely nauseated:

- **Step 1:** Drink clear regular sodas, such as 7Up, Sprite, or ginger ale (this is not the time for "diet" drinks), that have been allowed to go flat (keep in an open glass for a half hour). Consume no more than a 1/2 ounce at a time. Do this every five minutes for the first hour.

- **Step 2:** If you are able to tolerate this amount of liquids, increase to 1 ounce every five minutes for the next hour.
- **Step 3:** If you can tolerate this amount, you may now consume clear liquids ad lib.
- **Step 4:** You may try eating soft nonfat foods after four hours. Consume no more than 4 ounces in 15 minutes.

The National Hospital for Neurology and Neurosurgery in London set out to determine the proportion of migraine patients who could eat or drink at the beginning and height of a migraine attack, what they were able to eat, and the effects of those particular foods. This is what they found:[5]

- 54 percent could not take any food by mouth during this time.

Of the 46 percent who could eat:

- 8 percent could eat normally.
- 16 percent either took smaller amounts of their normal food intake or ate lighter meals.
- 76 percent found they could consume dry, carbohydrate-rich foods.

"If you only get infrequent migraines, then consume some caffeine from whatever source is your food of choice in order to stop them. Preferentially, have your caffeine with some sugar," notes Dr. Frederick Freitag of the Diamond Headache Clinic.

Q **How long should cold or frozen beverages or smoothies sit out at room temperature before consumption if a person is sensitive to them?**

The real trick is not to freeze your soft palate! Try to take small sips, keeping the liquid in your mouth until it has a chance to warm, and then swallow.

Brain Freeze No More

90 percent of migraine sufferers report sensitivity to ice cream and cold beverages.

How cold is your ice cream or iced coffee (decaf of course)? Cold enough to cause a brain freeze? During a brain freeze, the rapid cooling of an area on the roof of the mouth affects nerve endings that may then trigger headaches.

Because the majority of migraine sufferers appear to be particularly sensitive to cold foods and beverages, it's a good idea to:

- Let your ice-cold food or drink sit out at room temperature for about 10 minutes—just enough to take the edge off temperature-wise.

- Eat frozen foods more slowly than you normally would. You can warm each bite in your mouth first to give your palate time to adjust. This will also help you enjoy the food and savor the flavor more.

- If it seems like sipping cold or frozen beverages or smoothies from a straw makes it worse, try enjoying your shake or smoothie with a long spoon instead.

- Cold foods or drinks are more likely to trigger headaches if you are overheated from exercise or hot outdoor temperatures, so take the time to cool down before eating or drinking them.

Is there a connection between migraines and PMS?

The typical PMS complaints are very similar to early migraine symptoms (irritability, fatigue, food cravings, and so on), which might suggest there is some sort of connection between the two. But while we wait for more research to be conducted in this area, if your PMS symptoms are more severe, including premenstrual depression and mood lability, other measures may be required, so make sure to speak to your doctor about it.

Do you know of any diet or lifestyle changes to help prevent hormonal headaches?

According to Dr. Frederick Freitag of the Diamond Headache Clinic, the best bet here is to increase the amount of magnesium in the diet. This has been demonstrated to prevent menstrual migraines in controlled trials. (For a list of magnesium-rich foods, check out Step #10 of the Food Steps to Freedom in Chapter 4.)

Can We De-Stress Our Diet?

People with depression or anxiety have a higher risk of headaches than the general population, according to Dr. Lisa Mannix from the Diamond Headache Clinic. Talk to your physician about possible pharmacological options that may help these medical concerns.

The way I see it, stress and diet influence each other— the chicken and the egg both come first depending on the situation. Stress can lead some people to crave and eat (and overeat) junk food. While in other instances, eating an unhealthy diet rich in sugar, unhealthy fat, caffeine, and so on can lead some people to be more physically stressed or more likely to become stressed.

To de-stress our diet, we have to work on both ends of that stress stick. We have to find new ways to react to the stress in our lives, and we have to set ourselves up for de-stress success by eating a healthy diet on a regular basis—a diet designed to be rich in the nutrients that will help keep our mood up and our stress down.

Decreasing Underlying Stress

Ways to decrease underlying stress in our lives include:

- Try to find a healthy balance between the different aspects of your life, including family, work, and personal interests.

- Do you have a sense of purpose in your life? This brings many people an inner peace.

- Do you get enough sleep? Ample sleep helps your body recover from the day's stresses. Being overly tired can only exacerbate the stress we are feeling during the day.

- Don't smoke. Smoking is a stimulant and is addictive. It will only add to the level of stress in your life, as well as lower your body's immune system and decrease its ability to defend itself against illness and disease.

- Do you have the social support you need in your life? Do you feel as though you are loved and valued by your family, friends, and the community around you? Recent research suggests a strong association between social support and better mental and physical health.

Finding New Ways to Cope With Life's Stresses

Instead of counterproductive eating responses to stress in our lives, try and plug in as many of the following healthy coping strategies whenever possible. Find the ones that work best for you. Here are some things to do and think about that may make stress less likely to happen and make you more resistant to stress when it does strike:

- Are you exercising throughout the week? Physical activity can help reduce stress and your response to stress. There are two types of exercise that are particularly helpful: aerobic exercise (the type of exercise that increases your heart rate) and stretching (Pilates and yoga, for example), which relieves muscle tension.

- Note: A recent study adds to the evidence suggesting that a simple exercise program can improve mood (along with cardiovascular function). In this study of women with Alzheimer's disease, all of the subjects who participated in the eight-week exercise program, reported improvements in mood.[6]

- Don't let feelings such as fear, insecurity, anxiety, depression, or guilt trigger a stress response. You may need to seek professional help to learn how to stop negative thoughts and work through them in a more productive and healthful way.

- Writing as a release. Even if you don't think you are a "good writer," writing can help relieve stress and keep it from building up. Try writing for 10 to 15 minutes a day about any stressful events and how you felt about them.

- Just talk about it! Sometimes talking to a trusted friend or family member about your feelings or a situation at work or home can help more than you think. Think about lining up a de-stress buddy to call or e-mail when the going gets tough.

- Laugh therapy. Laughing, I mean really laughing, can be a powerful stress-reducer. Think about having some emergency humor on hand for those stressful times when you need your humor in a pinch. Can you make a cassette, DVD, or VHS tape of 10 to 15 minutes of one of your favorite comedians? In the time it takes to take a coffee break, you can be laughing away the stress of the day.

- Try biofeedback. Biofeedback is a method of consciously controlling a body function that is normally regulated by the body (blood pressure, heart rate, and muscle tension, for example). Biofeedback therapists teach you physical and mental exercises (using a monitoring device and sensors attached to your body) that help you control the function you are working on, such as reducing muscle tension. This therapy is a bit of a commitment though, because it takes most people about 12 sessions to have success with it. Biofeedback is mainly used to control problems related to stress or blood flow, such as headaches, high blood pressure, or sleep disorders.

The following are specific suggestions to help you focus on relaxing the body or certain parts of the body:

- **Muscle relaxation:** Reduces muscle tension by relaxing individual muscle groups.
- **Massage (particularly shoulder and neck massage):** Take a massage class with your spouse, friend, or coworker so you can come to each other's need on particularly stressful days.
- **Breathing exercises.**
- **Aromatherapy:** Aromatherapy can encourage calmness in some people. Aromatherapy ingredients come from essential oils in plants that appear to promote relaxation. They can be found in oils, lotions, and candles.
- **The following are specific suggestions to help you relax the mind:**

- **Guided imagery or meditation tapes.**
- **Hypnosis and self-hypnosis:** These techniques can help some people open the mind to suggestions that may relieve stress or change the way they react to stress.
- **Music:** Music can encourage calmness or improve your mood. The type of music is completely a personal thing. Some people feel calm listening to classical music; for others it might be uplifting country western music.

F.Y.I. Another Reason to Exercise

Exercise helps fight depression in two ways: by stimulating the production of endorphins (brain chemicals that produce feelings of well-being) and by activating the neurotransmitters (chemicals used by nerve cells to communicate with one another) associated with depression, namely serotonin and norepinephrine. When you experience depression, levels of serotonin or norepinephrine—or both—may be out of sync. Exercise may help synchronize these brain chemicals so that depression is perhaps less likely.

The Two Hormones Linking Food and Stress

The Happy Hormone

One key to the link between food and mood is serotonin, which I fondly nicknamed the "happy hormone." Serotonin is made in the brain from the amino acid tryptophan (found in dairy, animal, and fish protein) with the help of certain B vitamins. You would think that foods high in protein (amino acids are the building blocks of protein) would increase the levels of tryptophan, but it's actually the opposite. When eating foods high in protein, tryptophan has to fight with the other amino acids to cross the blood–brain barrier to get into the brain. (Tryptophan is the weaker of the amino acids, and generally only a small amount makes it into the brain when other amino acids are present.) But here's the catch: when you eat almost all carbs in a meal, it triggers insulin to clear the other amino acids from the bloodstream, which leaves tryptophan a smooth passage into the brain. This in turn boosts the serotonin level in the brain.

Following are a few key facts about serotonin:

1. High serotonin levels help boost your mood.
2. High serotonin levels help diminish food cravings.
3. High serotonin levels help increase your threshold for pain.
4. High serotonin levels help you feel calm and help you sleep.
5. Carbohydrate-rich meals boost levels of serotonin in the brain (eating a meal that contains any amount of protein decreases it).

The Stress Hormone

When you are stressed, your body releases more cortisol hormone into your bloodstream. Cortisol sends appetite-stimulating neurotransmitters into overdrive, while lowering levels of serotonin. This combination programs your brain to crave carbohydrate-rich foods. The carb-rich foods you then eat boost serotonin levels, which makes you calm again.

This certainly makes carbs sound like the good guys, doesn't it? And they are! But there is a way to give your body the carbohydrates it craves during stress without overdoing refined carbs from sugars and white flour products: complex or "whole" carbohydrate foods shall set you free! They give you the carbs you crave, along with fiber, vitamins, minerals, and phytochemicals galore.

De-Stress Your Diet

Some people tend to overeat all the wrong foods when they are stressed out. There are two problems here: the part about overeating and the part about eating the wrong foods. Keep in mind that eating a healthy, balanced, nutrient-rich diet is your best nutritional defense against stress. No high-priced vitamin supplements need apply. The answer is in your supermarket. There is more and more evidence in scientific literature suggesting that what we eat does in fact contribute to our moods, our stress levels, our brain functions, and our energy levels. Some of us already know this from our own personal experiences.

Todd Edwards, Ph.D., a family therapist and associate professor at the University of San Diego's School of Education, says he often finds a connection between a client's bad mood and his or her poor eating habits. That reminds me of the "garbage in, garbage out" catchphrase. The following information should help you get a better handle on making some healthful changes to de-stress your diet.

Keep Carbs Handy and Healthy

A study in 1995 (before the low-carb hysteria) looked at obese women who described themselves as people who eat excessive amounts of carbohydrate-rich foods when stressed. Participants were assigned to either a 1,350-calorie, carbohydrate-rich diet or a protein-rich diet for seven weeks. Interestingly, more women lost weight on the carbohydrate-rich diet. Yet perhaps more importantly, there was a decrease in carbohydrate cravings and an increase in vigor for those on the carbohydrate-rich diet.[7]

So while nixing carbs does not sound like the right answer, choosing your carbs wisely certainly is. We want the carbohydrate foods we choose to help nourish our body and have some staying power. Namely, we want foods with ample fiber. You won't find ample fiber in soda, cheese, or candy bars, but you will find it in fruits, vegetables, beans, and whole grains.

Omega-3s to the Rescue!

Although the uplifting effect of omega-3 fatty acids (found naturally in fish and certain plant foods, including canola oil and ground flaxseed) on mood and mood disorders hasn't been proven yet, there have been plenty of studies that suggest a strong connection. One recent study reported that it may not be "the more the merrier" in the case of omega-3 supplements. This Harvard Medical School trial found that depressed patients improved more on a supplement of 1 gram per day of DHA (docosahexaenoic acid) than on 2 or 4 grams a day. One of the researchers, Dr. Mischoulon, speculated that it may be the ratio between the omega-3s and the omega-6s that is the key factor. Eating more omega-3 rich foods and switching to cooking fats that are higher in omega-3 and lower in omega-6 (canola oil, for example) certainly makes sense for a lot of health reasons, and now uplifting our mood can be added to it.[8]

Another recent study with the omega-3 fatty acid found in fish, EPA (eicosapentaenoic acid), reported improvements in all measures of depression in those taking fish oil supplements (1 gram per day) plus medication, compared to those taking a placebo plus medication.[9]

Why does a helpful effect of omega-3s on mood and depression make scientific sense?

1. In areas of the world where more omega-3s are consumed, depression is less prevalent.

2. Depression rates are high among alcoholics and postpartum patients (both groups tend to be omega-3 deficient).

3. Omega-3 fatty acids are depleted in the red blood cells of people with depression compared to controls.

Cut the Caffeine!

Some people are sensitive to caffeine. You probably know who you are. Drinking just one caffeinated coffee or soda makes you jittery, light-headed, or feeling like your blood sugar has hit an all-time low. I know of what I speak. I went "decaf" many years ago for good reason. Just a half a cup of caffeinated coffee in the evening will keep me up for half the night.

Caffeine is a stimulant. It stimulates the bowels and the bladder, and it does seem to increase your energy level for the short term. But what goes up must come down—and in susceptible people, it can come crashing down. Larry Christensen, Ph.D., a researcher with the University of South Alabama, has found in recent studies that when people sensitive to caffeine eliminate caffeine from their diet, their mood and energy levels significantly improve. Not sure if you are a caffeine-sensitive person? Try avoiding it for a few weeks and see if there's a difference in the way you feel. But it's difficult for some people to go cold turkey on caffeine, so taper off your caffeine intake a cup a day until you are down to none. (More on caffeine in the Food Steps to Freedom in Chapter 4.)

Additional Diet Tips to De-Stress Your Diet

The following are additional tips to help you de-stress your diet and avoid headaches:

- Try eating smaller, more frequent meals throughout the day rather than three big meals. It can provide your body with a consistent supply of energy and help you avoid feeling tired or overly hungry.

- You're not skipping breakfast, are you? When people eat breakfast, they tend to have more consistent moods and are less likely to suffer food cravings later in the day. If you are one of those people who aren't quite ready to eat first thing in the morning, plan or bring a high-fiber morning snack with you for when your stomach awakens. Try to include some protein in your breakfast selection, too, and minimize high-sugar breakfast foods if you can.

- Are you drinking alcohol? Alcohol is not a healthy or effective way to relax or relieve stress. Even though many people think it does the opposite, alcohol is actually a depressant. And overdrinking only adds to the stress in your life.

- Are you eating for all the right reasons? Are you eating when you are truly hungry, and stopping when you are comfortable? If not, try and understand why that may be. What else may be driving your impulse to eat?

- Chart your mood and food intake over a week. Consider how your mood changes in relation to the food you have or have not eaten. Do you come home from work irritable and ready to explode? Does this have something to do with making poor mealtime choices or eating little or nothing for lunch?

- Try making a beneficial dietary change. Try it, you might like it! You know the saying "you don't know until you try it"? Well, that's true here as well.

Q

Is there such a thing as "good mood" foods?

I know, I know, this is a book about diet and headaches. But because many people who suffer from chronic headaches also suffer from forms of depression, and because lowering your stress level can help discourage headaches, it makes sense to take some time to talk about what we can eat to boost our mood. Because you are interested in making some diet and lifestyle changes to help your headaches anyway (thus you're reading this book), what a great time to talk about "good mood" foods.

But can you really eat certain foods to keep bad moods at bay and good moods plentiful? There is still much for the scientific community to learn about when it comes to how our diet influences our moods. While we don't have the whole story yet, we certainly have some clues that are pointing us in the right direction.

Recent studies have shown that there are a number of things we can do foodwise to help stabilize our moods. I advise trying to incorporate as many of the following food suggestions as possible into your diet so that you have all your food-mood ducks in a row. The following food suggestions also happen to offer many additional health benefits to your body in general, so you have nothing to lose in the health department either.

7 Things You Can Do Today to Elevate Your Mood Tomorrow (And Beyond)

1. Work More Omega-3 Fatty Acids Into Your Diet

Researchers have noted that omega-3 polyunsaturated fatty acids, found in fish and some plant sources, may be mood stabilizers, playing a role in mental well-being.

A recent study that looked at New Zealanders ages 15 and older found that fish consumption was significantly associated with higher self-reported mental health status, even after the researchers adjusted for other factors that could have influenced the results.

A recent review of data on the prevalence of postpartum depression found that lower levels of DHA (the omega-3 fatty acid in fish) content in mother's breast milk and lower seafood consumption by the mother were both associated with higher rates of postpartum depression.

Eating plant foods rich in omega-3s is also probably a good idea. The top few plant foods include: ground flax-seed (1 tablespoon a day is considered a safe and effective dose for most people, but check with your doctor if you have concerns), canola oil, purslane, cauliflower, red kidney beans, and broccoli.

2. Eat a Balanced Breakfast

Eat a breakfast every morning that includes lots of fiber, nutrients, some lean protein, and good fats to help balance out the whole grain carbohydrates.

According to some researchers, eating breakfast regularly leads to improved moods, better memory, and more energy throughout the day, as well as feelings of calmness.

3. Eat More Selenium-Rich Foods

Selenium is a mineral the brain can count on. Studies have reported an association between low selenium intake and poorer moods. Although the underlying mechanism is unclear, researchers do have some clues. The metabolism of selenium by the brain differs from other organs in that, in times of deficiency, the brain retains selenium to a greater extent. This leads some researchers to believe selenium plays an important function in the brain

The top selenium-rich food sources (not including organ meats, which are also shockingly high in cholesterol) include brazil nuts, oysters, albacore tuna, clams, sardines, pork tenderloin, crab, saltwater fish, whole wheat pasta, lean pork chops, chicken meat (dark and light), regular pasta, lean lamb, sunflower seeds, whole wheat bread, plain bagels, brown rice, oatmeal, flour tortillas, soy nuts, fresh-water fish, eggs, low-fat cottage cheese, tofu, pinto beans, and low-fat yogurt.

4. If You Are Overweight, Lose Weight Slowly But Surely

Some researchers advise that slow weight reduction in overweight women can help to elevate mood. Fad dieting isn't the answer though, because depriving yourself of too many calories and carbohydrates can help instigate irritability.

5. Eat More Folate-Rich Foods

Not enough folic acid in our diet can cause lower levels of serotonin in our brain and low moods. Some studies suggest that folate supplements (there is a day's supply in most balanced multivitamins) and emphasizing folate-rich fruits and vegetables may be helpful in some depressed patients. Folate-rich foods include spinach, green soybeans, lentils, romaine lettuce, pinto beans, black beans, navy beans, kidney beans, broccoli, asparagus, greens, orange juice, beets, papaya, Brussels sprouts, and tofu.

F.Y.I. Tryptophan

Tryptophan is a nonessential amino acid. As more tryptophan enters the brain, more serotonin is synthesized in the brain, and our mood improves. Will eating foods high in tryptophan help? Tryptophan is in almost all protein-rich foods. But other amino acids are better at getting into the brain from the bloodstream, which is why eating carbohydrates seems to help tryptophan's chances of crossing the blood–brain barrier.

---

6. Go Carbs Go! (But in Moderation)

Carbohydrate-rich meals increase brain tryptophan and serotonin levels in rats while protein-rich meals decrease them. Some researchers suggest that carbohydrate-rich meals may have an effect on our moods due to other mechanisms in addition to changes in brain serotonin, including comforting feelings and memories associated with eating these foods in our youth.

When it comes to raising serotonin, there is one type of nutrition component that is almost always mentioned—carbohydrates. It is common knowledge to mood experts that carbohydrate consumption increases serotonin release and that protein intake doesn't. This can be a double-edged sword for carbohydrates though. This means we need carbohydrates, yes; however, it behooves us to choose our carbohydrates wisely. The focus should be on carbohydrate foods that come with lots of nutrients and fiber, as well as the carbohydrate calories. Such foods include whole grains, beans, fruits, and vegetables.

While carbohydrates do increase serotonin, thereby boosting your mood, this also means that many of us may have developed a tendency to overconsume carbohydrates in an effort to make ourselves feel better.

Dr. Judith Wurtman, a researcher with the MIT Department of Brain and Cognitive Sciences and Clinical Research Center, as well as a national expert on the issue of food and mood, suspects that many women learn to overeat carbohydrates (particularly snack foods such as chips or pastries) that are rich in carbs and fats to make themselves feel better. Using or abusing certain foods as though they are drugs is probably a major cause of weight gain for some susceptible women.

NOTE:

Someone with persistent depression should seek medical help from a professional, such as a psychologist, psychiatrist, or social worker. If you are not sure where to turn, ask your physician for a referral. Check your employee benefits for something called the "Employee Assistance Plan," which offers free counseling. Keep in mind that depression is more treatable today than ever before due to progress in medications and psychological counseling techniques.

Chapter 4

The 10 Food Steps to Freedom

There is a lot of helpful information for you in this book, some specific to your type of headache and some more general information. But let's face it, most of us need to be given specific (preferably practical) things we can do today. So here are the 10 Food Steps to Freedom.

Keep in mind, though, that there can probably never be complete freedom from headaches. Our goal is to decrease your number of headaches and the length and severity of your headaches if possible. These are 10 food steps that seem to help most people suffering from headaches and migraines, although feel free to add any steps you think apply to you and your specific headaches or food triggers.

Bottom line, as you read about the 10 Food Steps to Freedom, take to heart that the general theme here is to eat a healthy diet—the way we all know we should eat, but somehow never do. We also need to cook at home more, and eat at fast-food chains less. We need to choose more "whole" foods, and less processed and refined foods.

Step #1: Keep a Headache Diary: Be Your Own Food Detective

Keeping a headache diary is listed as Food Step #1 for good reason: this is perhaps the most important tool in "freeing" you from headaches (as much as possible anyway). Information is power, and the only way to know what foods, beverages, or eating habits (such as skipping meals) may be triggering your headaches is to write everything down and connect the dots.

Headaches are a highly individual disease. This means you need to find the specific foods, eating patterns, or other changes that appear to be your personal headache triggers. Only then can you begin to prevent some of your headaches.

The headache diary may also enable you to figure out what environmental changes seem to set you off (changing altitudes, air pollution, climates, and so on), which may lead you and your doctor to try prophylactic medications and make prophylactic dietary changes the next time you anticipate being in that same situation.

Keeping a headache diary may be a bit of a hassle, but it will help you identify your headache triggers be it your:

- Exercise habits.
- Sleep habits.
- Menstrual cycle.
- Emotional stress.
- Eating style and food habits.
- Specific foods and beverages.
- Environmental changes.

Include Amount of Food and Drink

I know it's a pain to write down approximately how much you eat or drink of certain items in your diary, but there is a method to my madness. Remember the second complication of migraine headaches from Chapter 3? A migraine response to a food or drink trigger may depend on how much of the food or drink is consumed. Well, writing down how much you consume of certain possible triggers is your way of uncovering what amounts tend to do you in.

Just a Reminder

A headache may not come about for several hours to several days after eating a trigger food. This makes it a lot more difficult to find connections between eating or drinking certain items and a migraine. In your diary, you can go back and chart how long before your headache you ate or drank a possible trigger food or drink. Write the number of hours from when you ate the possible trigger food to when you started having your migraine next to the trigger food in your diary. Over the course of several weeks, you may start seeing a connection or pattern.

6 Keys to Keeping Your Headache Diary

1. Keep your headache diary for one to four weeks, depending on the frequency of your headaches. Keep it longer if you find it helps you and makes you feel better.

2. Review the foods you ate and other eating habits (spacing of meals, for example) up to 72 hours before you experienced each headache.

3. Review any changes in stress, sleep, exercise, and so on. Changes in daily activities can trigger a migraine, too.

4.   Identify any patterns that may be triggering your headaches.

5.   If you suspect a particular food to be a trigger, eliminate it as best as possible for one to four weeks, depending on the frequency of your headaches, to see if it seems to help.

6.   If eliminating a particular food or drink from your diet seems to help reduce the frequency of your headaches, when it is convenient, try eating it again to see if it triggers one. If it does, you should probably consider avoid that particular food or drink in the future.

And now without further ado . . . your unofficial headache diary! (Use the template on pages 81–83 to create your own headache diary.)

F.Y.I. Try Exercising

Aerobic exercise, the kind of constant moving exercise that works your cardiovascular and respiratory system (swimming, walking, and cycling, for example), has been shown to help reduce headaches in some people. Exercising also makes you feel better about yourself and your body. It helps you feel stronger and healthier, and that can be a very powerful medicine no matter what your ailment. Even briskly walking 20 minutes a day can benefit your body and mind. Just make sure to check with your doctor before starting any exercise program.

Headache Diary

Date of headache/migraine:

Any warning signs that a headache/migraine was coming:

Time headache started:

Time headache ended:

Describe the type of headache pain (piercing or throbbing, for example):

Describe the intensity of head pain: (circle one)
(low intensity) 1 2 3 4 5 6 7 8 9 10 (high intensity)

Location of pain (between the eyes or back of head, for example):

Any treatment or medication taken:

How did the treatment work for you:

How many hours did you sleep the night before and the night before that?

Night before: _____hours

Night before that: _____hours

Did you exercise today or yesterday?

Today: Type of exercise:

How long: _____minutes

Yesterday: Type of exercise:

How long: _____minutes

What did you eat today? (List the times of your meals or snacks so you can see whether the spacing or skipping of meals may be part of the problem.)

Time:

Time:

Time:

Time:

Time:

What did you eat the day before? (Symptoms can develop up to 24 hours and beyond after eating certain foods, so that's why it is helpful to know what you ate the day before.)

Time:

Time:

Time:

Time:

Time:

Were there any events or changes a day or two before the headache (stress, travel, change in weather, for example)?

Any suspected triggers or connections based on the above?

Step #2: Eat When You Are Hungry, Stop When You Are Comfortable, and Avoid Skipping Meals

Sue, a busy accountant, has learned to eat the right foods at the right times. Sue knows by experience that it is essential she eat a breakfast balanced with some protein and eat lunch on time, too: "If I skip either meal, I can expect a headache. I get crabby and lose my concentration, and my work suffers."

This sounds pretty simple, doesn't it: eat when you are hungry, and stop when you are comfortable. It's anything but. We are born doing this instinctively, but as we grow older we begin to mess with this simple formula. Some of us have a hard time eating when we are hungry—either we eat when we aren't really hungry, or we forget to eat even though we are hungry because we get caught up in work and other activities. Others have a hard time with the other end of this commonsense equation—they can't stop eating when they are comfortable. Believe it or not, there are people who forget to eat, who somehow are able to ignore the emptiness in their stomachs. While people trying to lose or maintain weight might consider these people lucky, it can be a hazard if you suffer from headaches.

Making sure to eat when you are hungry is the part that is most helpful to discouraging headaches and migraines. The reason I also mention overeating is because if you stop when you are comfortable and not overeat, you are more likely to eat when you are hungry again. Overeating can make some people feel like they've been "bad" and they need to make up for overeating earlier by starving themselves later.

The most important meal not to skip is breakfast because breakfast is the first meal after a possible 13-hour fast (if 6 P.M.

is the last time you ate and 7 A.M. is the first time you eat again). If you aren't keen on eating first thing in the morning, that's OK. You need to plan ahead, though, and bring along your breakfast to eat sometime later in the morning when your body is ready to eat. This actually describes me to a T. Because I work from home, I make myself a plate or bowl of whatever breakfast item I have cooked or prepared for my two girls that morning, but put it aside or in the refrigerator. I take my girls to school and do an hour or so of work, and then lo and behold, I'm ready to eat right around 9 or 10 A.M. It's easy because my breakfast is already made (although I have to warm certain items up in the microwave).

What Is Hunger Exactly?

Hunger is the feeling your body has when it needs food. It can include:[1]

- Stomach growls.
- Stomach aches.
- Weakness.
- Headaches.
- Dizziness.
- Anxiety.
- Loss of concentration.
- Food cravings.
- Mouth watering.

4 Keys to Eating When You Are Hungry

1. Stay tuned to what your body is telling you about your physical hunger. Get to know what your empty stomach and early hunger feels like so you can respond to it in time.

2. Organize your morning so that you have plenty of time to enjoy your first meal of the day. This is purely individual, but for some this might include making breakfast or part of breakfast the night before. Taking your shower at night so you aren't taking it in the morning and having what you are going to wear pressed and ready to go will give you more time so that you won't rush through breakfast.

3. Come prepared so that when hunger strikes, you can nourish your body with healthy snack and meal options. Have some healthy snacks to tide you over stored in various strategic places, such as your purse or briefcase, your car, or your desk at work.

4. Be aware that caffeine can seem to bring on hunger quickly in some people. Caffeine is a stimulant, and although it generally buzzes you with quick-start energy, it can cause a reactive low blood sugar in some people (myself included).

Avoiding Hypoglycemia

Your brain and body require a constant supply of energy in the blood. Eating small, frequent meals throughout the day (and at the very least, not skipping meals) is likely to keep your blood sugar and energy stable. When you eat small, frequent meals, you are more likely to prevent low blood sugar levels, which can trigger headaches, irritability, food cravings, and so on, in susceptible people.

Hypoglycemia is a fancy word for "low" (hypo) "blood sugar" (glycemia), and it happens when the level of sugar or glucose in your bloodstream drops too low to fuel the body. There are two types of hypoglycemia. The one that we are talking about here is called "fasting hypoglycemia." Fasting hypoglycemia occurs when you haven't eaten for many hours. It is a potential headache trigger that we definitely can do something about: eat when you are hungry and do your best not to skip meals. (Check out the portable snack ideas in Chapter 6.)

Step #3: Limit Caffeine Intake or Eliminate It Completely. And When You Do Cut Back, Do It Gradually

It can get rather confusing for a headache sufferer because the truth is that caffeine is often helpful in treating acute migraine attacks. It's one of the active ingredients in many headache medications (over-the-counter and prescription). But there are two ways that caffeine can actually cause headaches:

1. When you drink an excessive amount of caffeine.
2. When your body is having "withdrawal" from your daily caffeine intake.

Experts also advise headache sufferers to avoid caffeine-containing products while taking a pain-relieving medication, especially medication that already contains caffeine.

Are You Having Caffeine Withdrawal Headaches?

The blood vessels seem to become sensitized to caffeine, and when the caffeine is suddenly not consumed, a headache may occur within less than 24 hours. And occur it does. My husband, who is good for about two big cups of caffeinated coffee a day during his workday, cannot go one Saturday or Sunday without at least one cup of caffeinated coffee. If he does skip his coffee in the morning, a headache will be knocking on his door by lunchtime.

Caffeine Content of Common Medications[2]

Over-the-Counter Medications

Drug Name	Caffeine Content Per Dose (mgs)
Actamin Super	65.4
Anacin, Maximum Strength	32
Anacin, Regular Strength	32
Bayer Select Maximum Strength Headache Pain Relief	65.4
Dristan	16
Excedrin, Extra Strength	65
Excedrin, Regular Strength	65
Goody's Extra Strength Tablets	16.25
Goody's Headache Powder	32.5
Midol, Cramps & Body Aches	32.4
Midol, Menstrual Complete	60
NoDoz	32.4
Vanquish Caplets	33
Vivarin	200

Prescription Medications

Drug Name	Caffeine Content Per Dose (mgs)
Cafergot Suppositories	100
Cafergot Tablets	100
Darvon Compound	32.4
Florinal Capsules and Tablets	40
Florinal With Codeine	40
Norgesic	30
Norgesic Forte	60
Triaminicin With Codein	30

Note: All drugs containing caffeine are not included in this list. Always check the labels of over-the-counter medications for the caffeine content and ask your pharmacist about the caffeine content of prescription medications.

Caffeine Content of Common Beverages of Foods

Coffee

Beverage	Caffeine Content (mgs)
Cappuccino, double, 1 cup	120
Cappucino, regular, 1 cup	60
Coffee, regular, 1 cup	138
Coffee drink, sweetened mocha, 1 cup	87
Espresso, 1/4 cup	120
Latte, double (iced or hot), 1 cup	120
Latte, regular (iced or hot), 1 cup	60

Tea

Beverage	Caffeine Content (mgs)
Nestea Iced Tea, Earl Grey, 1 cup	33
Nestea Iced Tea, Lemon (sweetened/low cal), 1 cup	11
Tea, brewed (hot)	47

Soda

Beverage	Caffeine Content (mgs)
Cola, regular or diet, 12-oz. can	42
Mountain Dew, 12-oz. can	52
Surge, 12-oz. can	48

Chocolate

Beverage	Caffeine Content (mgs)
Chocolate, semisweet, 1 oz.	18
Chocolate milk, 1 cup	5
Chocolate milkshake, 1 cup	5
Cocoa powder (processed with alkali), 1 tbs.	4
Cocoa powder, 1 tbs.	12
Hot cocoa. regular, 1 packet	5
Nestle Crunch, 1.4-oz. bar	10
Snickers, 2-oz. bar	4

The following findings are from a first-of-its-kind research program led by Johns Hopkins University professor Roland Griffiths that took into account more than 60 studies on caffeine withdrawal[3]:

- Half of all adults experience drug-withdrawal symptoms when their caffeinated coffee or soft-drink supply is suddenly cut off.
- 13 percent of adults who suddenly have to go without caffeine become such physical messes, they can't work or socialize.
- 90 percent of American adults are using caffeine.

If a substance causes withdrawal symptoms in people, it implies addiction. And we know that caffeine is a stimulant and that the human body can become addicted to it, whether you are addicted to one cup of a caffeinated beverage in the morning or six cups throughout the day. There are worse things to be addicted to, yes. But this is an addiction you can easily kick, and your motivation is that it will most likely help with your headaches.

Caffeine-withdrawal symptoms included:

- Headaches (sometimes debilitating).
- Fatigue or drowsiness.
- Depression or irritability.
- Difficulty concentrating.
- Flu-like aches and nausea.

How to Cut Caffeine Without Withdrawal Symptoms

You can avoid all of the listed caffeine-withdrawal symptoms by cutting back slowly on your caffeine intake each day. The goal is to taper off your caffeine consumption to zero over the course of several weeks.

5 Steps to Being Caffeine-Free and Withdrawal-Free!

For example, if you normally drink three tall cups of coffee a day, you can:

1. Cut total consumption to two tall cups a day for a few days.

2. Drink one caffeinated cup of coffee and one cup of half caffeinated–half decaf coffee for a few days or a week.

3. Drink one caffeinated cup of coffee and one cup of decaf coffee for a few days or a week.

4. Drink one cup of half caffeinated–half decaf coffee and one cup of decaf coffee for a few days or a week.

5. Drink two cups of decaf coffee a day for whatever length of time you choose.

Step #4: Avoid Eating a High-Fat Diet

A significant decrease in migraines was observed when dietary fat consumption was cut in half. Another study noted improvements when patients reduced the total fat in their diets to 20 to 28 grams a day. I can't say I'm surprised. Avoiding a high-fat diet keeps popping up as the "preferred way of eating" no matter what medical condition I'm writing about (IBS, acid reflux, diabetes, and so on). Eating a healthy, lower-fat diet is also the best way to eat if you want to reduce your risk of heart disease, many types of cancer, and obesity. What more reason do you need?

Frankly, I could write an entire book on how best to avoid a high-fat diet. Oh, yeah . . . I already have! If you are interested, check out my latest book titled *Fry Light, Fry Right* (Black Dog & Leventhal, 2004). But to help get you started right now, let's take a look at where most of the fat in the typical American diet is coming from, and then work backwards.

Avoid Hidden Fats

A recent analysis of USDA consumption data on U.S. adults from 1994 to 1996 suggests that we need to do a better job of avoiding hidden fats in meat mixtures and grain products. Based on this data, the following table, listing different food categories and what percentage of fat they contribute, gives you a good idea of where the fat in our diets is really coming from.[4]

Food Category	% of Total Fat Contributed
Grains	27%
Grain mixtures (pasta dishes, pizza, etc.)	9%
Pastries (cakes, cookies, pies, etc.)	7%
Grain snacks (crackers, salty snacks, etc.)	3%
Vegetables (includes potatoes and potato products)	10%
Dairy (milk, cheese, yogurt, etc.)	13%
Meats	30%
Meat mixture (hamburgers, fish, poultry, etc.)	11.5%
Eggs (includes foods containing mostly eggs)	3%
Nuts/Legumes	3.5%
Fats/Oils (butter, margarine, salad dressings, etc.)	10%
Sugar/Sweets (includes candy)	2%

Know Where the Fat Comes From

The initital diets of women participating in the Women's Health Initiative Low-Fat Dietary Modification Trial were analyzed, and the percentage of fat contributed by various food groups was calculated. The winning food group, "Added Fats," contributed a whopping 25 percent of the total fat taken in, followed by "Meats" with 21 percent. "Desserts" ran up around 13 percent, and the "Milk and Cheese" group accounted for almost 10 percent. Take a look at the following table for the percentage of fat contributed by food groups and specific foods within each category, but remember, these percentages are only for women![5]

Food Groups	% Fat Intake
Added Fats	25%
Butter, margarine, oil, gravies, and sauces	34%
Mayonnaise	29%
Salad dressing	19%
Peanut butter and nuts	19%
Guacamole	.4%
Meats	21%
Beef, pork, lamb, and liver	43%
Hot dogs and luncheon meats	17%
Chicken	15.5%
Eggs	13.5%
Fish	7%
Bacon and sausage	4%
Desserts	13%
Doughnuts, cakes, and pastries	25%
Ice cream	24%
Chocolate candy	22%
Cookies	15%
Pies	13%
Milk and Cheese	10%
Cheese	67%
Milk	31%
Yogurt	2%

Food Groups	% Fat Intake
Mixed Dishes and Soups	10%
Pastas and pizza	45.5%
Stews and chili	32%
Mexican and Asian mixed dishes	12%
Soups	11%
High-Fat Breads and Salty Snacks	6%
Crackers, chips, and popcorn	44%
Biscuits, cornbread, and tortillas	35%
Fried potatoes and vegetables	18%
Waffles and pancakes	2%

10 Quick Ways to Eat a Lower-Fat Diet

Given what we have just learned, here are 10 quick ways to start eating a lower-fat diet.

1. Switch to reduced-fat milk, fat-free half-and-half, light ice cream, low-fat or nonfat cottage cheese, light or fat-free sour cream, and reduced-fat yogurt. Try to use these lower-fat options in your recipes.

2. Use reduced-fat cheese in your recipes. If you choose to use regular-fat cheese, try to cut the amount that you use in half. Either way, you cut the fat in half.

3. Choose leaner cuts of beef, processed meat, and pork. Try to cook and prepare the meat without adding a lot of fat (if any), and eat smaller portions of red meat. Tall order, I know, but it can be done!

4. Take the skin off your poultry before you cook it if possible, and cook your poultry without adding a lot of fat to keep it lean.

5. Use a half egg–half egg substitute mixture in your egg-based recipes.

6. Use less fat in your baking recipes whenever possible, and switch to canola oil or a margarine with no trans fats when possible. (When you take fat out, you have to add something healthy back in to replace the lost moisture and volume. Read on to find some smart substitution ideas!)

7. Choose reduced-fat crackers, chips, frozen entrées, and so on, whenever possible. This entails reading lots and lots of labels. But take heart: Once you read the labels and you find the best food choices, you won't have to read them again.

8. Choose grilled or oven-baked foods instead of deep-fried foods when possible.

9. Choose reduced-fat versions or use less of notorious high-fat ingredients such as mayonnaise, margarine, and salad dressing.

10. Use less fat and oil in cooking or when stir-frying, and switch to canola oil, olive oil, or no-trans margarine when possible.

Trim Back the Fat

Healthy food isn't going to do anyone any good if no one is eating it. That's been my motto for the 15 years or so that I've been lightening recipes. In other words, even if it's light in fat, its gotta taste great.

Five key ways to successfully trim back on fat in recipes are:

1. Find the ideal fat threshold for the recipe. How much can you cut without compromising flavor and texture?

2. Use the fat substitute that works best in that recipe.

3. Review the functions of each fat before you make changes to your recipe. When fat serves an irreplaceable function, you'll probably need to keep some of it in. But my experience has been, depending on the recipe, that you can usually cut it in half.

4. Substitute reduced-fat ingredients and products when appropriate. For example, use reduced-fat sharp cheddar instead of regular; use a good-tasting fat-free or light sour cream instead of regular; or use fat-free half-and-half instead of regular.

5. Change to a cooking method that eliminates the need for cooking fat (broiling, roasting, poaching, and steaming, for example) when possible. But when it is necessary to maintain the character of the food, do use a cooking method that involves fat—just use less of it.

Smart Substitutions

Based on two decades of experimentation with the best ways to lighten recipes, I've discovered there are ideal fat thresholds that you must keep for flavor. So if you cut back the fat in a particular recipe, you'll need a "fat replacement"—an extra ingredient you can add to help replace the fat you have taken out.

For example, if you are making a brownie recipe and you cut the butter back from 8 tablespoons to 3, you can add 5 tablespoons fat-free sour cream to the batter to make up the difference. Or if you are making a spice cake using a cake mix, don't add the 1/2 cup of oil the recipe requires. Instead add 1/2 cup of unsweetened applesauce (or some other fat replacement) instead.

Ideal Fat Thresholds and Substitution Table

Recipe	Fat Threshold	Fat Replacements
Biscuits/Scones	4 tbs. shortening for every 2 cups flour.	Fat-free cream cheese, nonfat or light sour cream, or flavored yogurt.
Cake Mixes	No additional fat is needed because most mixes already contain plenty.	Instead of adding the oil called for on the box, add applesauce, liqueur, fruit juice, flavored yogurt, or nonfat sour cream, depending on the type of cake.
Brownies	2 tbs. canola oil or butter per 4 oz. unsweetened chocolate and about 14 Tbs. flour.	Fat-free sour cream works well, as well as espresso or strong coffee.
Homemade Cakes and Coffee Cakes	1/4 to 1/3 cup fat ingredient per cake.	Try liqueur for some cakes, and light sour cream for chocolate cakes. Fruit puree and juice work well with carrot, apple, and spice cakes.
Cheese Sauce	No butter is needed, so omit it if it is called for (the cheese is the vital fatty ingredient). Use a reduced-fat cheddar.	Make your thickening paste by mixing the flour with a little bit of milk, then whisk in the remaining milk called for in the recipe.

Ideal Fat Thresholds and Substitution Table

Recipe	Fat Threshold	Fat Replacements
Cookies	Generally you can only cut the fat by half. If the original recipe calls for 1 cup of butter, for example, try cutting it to 2/3 to 1/2 cup.	Try fat-free cream cheese for rich cookies. Some fruit purees may work in fruit and drop cookies.
Marinades	1 tbs. of canola oil per cup of marinade (or none at all).	Fruit juices or beer help to balance the sharpness of the more acidic ingredients in a marinade, such as vinegar or tomato juice.
Muffins and Nut Breads	2 tbs. oil for a 12-muffin recipe.	Fat-free sour cream, low-fat flavored yogurts, fruit juice, and fruit purees (raspberry or pear) work well.
Vinaigrette Dressings	1 to 2 tbs. olive oil or canola oil per 1/2-cup of dressing.	Wine or champagne, fruit juice, and fruit purees (raspberry or pear) work well.
White Sauces and Gravies	1 tsp. butter per serving of sauce.	Simply add a little more milk. (Use whole milk or fat-free half-and-half for a rich white sauce.)

Bonus Tips

Here are four more substitution or fat-reduction tips to use when cooking various dishes:

1. Many recipes call for using a lot more oil or butter in panfrying or sautéing than is really necessary. Using a teaspoon of olive oil or canola oil, at most, usually does the trick.

2. Canola or olive oil cooking sprays help grease bakeware, cookware, and food surfaces with a minimal amount of fat.

3. If you can switch to canola or olive oil instead of using fat or shortening in a recipe, do it! These oils contain better fats (omega-3s) than the saturated fats found in shortening, butter, and stick margarines.

4. When you really need or want to use margarine, there are a few brands out there that have no or low amounts of trans fats (1 gram or less per tablespoon) and have less total fat per tablespoon than other products (8 grams of fat per tablespoon). Plus, they actually taste pretty good. The two that I tend to use are Take Control and Land O'Lakes Fresh Buttery Taste Spread.

Step #5: Switch to Plant and Fish Sources of Omega-3 Fatty Acids

Supplementing your diet with omega-3 fatty acids may be beneficial for headache management. We don't know this for sure yet, and some experts might say this is a bit of a stretch, but it's a good overall healthy thing to do. Omega-3s not only play a vital role in the health of the membrane of every cell in our bodies, they also help protect us from a number of key health threats. Boosting your omega-3 fatty acids from fish and plants will also help keep your mood high, your joints less inflamed, and your risk of heart disease low. It's a win, win, win situation.

Just how do omega-3s perform so many health "miracles" in people? One way, experts say, is by encouraging the production of body chemicals that help control inflammation in the joints, tissues, and blood vessels.

All you need to do is start enjoying a couple of servings a week of omega-3-rich fish, a few tablespoons a week of ground flaxseed, switch to canola oil in your cooking (canola oil has the highest amount of omega-3 fatty acids of the common cooking oils), and use as many products high in omega-3s in your cooking as possible.

How to Get What You Need

Omega-3 fatty acids are not one single nutrient, but a collection of several, including eicosapentaenoic acid (EPA) and docosahexaenoic acid (DHA). Both are found in greatest abundance in coldwater fish.

The recommendation for omega-3s is two servings of fish a week, which is well below the FDA's safe limit (due to concerns over mercury levels) of 12 ounces per week if each serving is about 3 to 4 ounces. It's best to eat a variety of fish, including salmon, tuna, and mackerel.

But even if you don't like fish or choose not to eat it, you can still get what you need from other dietary sources. The answer lies in plants rich in omega-3s, particularly flaxseed. Ground flaxseed is quite possibly the most potent plant source of plant omega-3s. It's rich in an omega-3 known as alpha-linolenic acid (ALA), which the body can convert to EPA and DHA (less than 5 percent of the ALA is converted). ALA also offers its own health benefits, including helping to boost the immune system and possibly protecting against recurrence of heart attacks. ALA may also have a possible anti-inflammatory effect on patients with rheumatoid arthritis, offer cardiovascular benefits different from fish omega-3s, and reduce breast tumor growth (in animals).

Ground flaxseed is a better choice over flax oil because it also contains 3 grams of fiber per tablespoon, as well as protective phytoestrogens. For more information and recipes for ground flaxseed, check out my book titled *The Flax Cookbook* (Marlowe & Company, 2003).

Other sources of plant omega-3s include canola oil, broccoli, cantaloupe, kidney beans, spinach, grape leaves, Chinese cabbage, cauliflower, and walnuts.

Just the Flax Please!

If you haven't heard a lot about flaxseed yet, then consider this your flaxseed wake-up call. Flaxseed is an actual "seed" grown mainly in Canada and in the Dakota states. It looks like brown sesame seeds. There is a lighter-colored type of flaxseed called golden flax, too. Flaxseed has been around for thousands of years, and when ground (you need to grind it before you eat it, otherwise it passes through your system and you don't get a chance to absorb any of its nutritional attributes) it basically looks a little like wheat germ. It has a nutty, pleasant flavor too.

What's Good About Flax?

Flaxseed has basically four major nutritional attributes:

1. It's one of the most potent food sources of plant omega-3 fatty acids.
2. It's one of the most potent sources of the plant estrogen (phytoestrogen) called lignans.

3. There are about 3 grams of fiber (1/3 soluble and 2/3 insoluble) per tablespoon of ground flaxseed.

4. It contains an antioxidant known as SDG (secoisolariciresinol diglycoside).

Why Ground Flaxseed Is the Way to Go

Ground flaxseed is what you want. Whole flax just passes through your system ("supplementing the sewer," as I say).

Flax oil or capsules only contain the plant omega-3s, and not the fiber or the plant estrogens that you get in ground flaxseed. Plus, I'm not sure about the safety of flax oil or capsules. I am comfortable with ground flaxseed in the dose of 1 to 2 tablespoons a day as part of a healthy diet.

You can find whole golden flax or regular flax in bulk at your health food store (you'll have to grind it yourself with a coffee grinder and keep it in a plastic bag in your freezer). You can also find it already ground (usually called flaxmeal) in bags at some grocery stores.

What's the Ideal Daily Dose of Flax?

"One to 2 tablespoons of ground flaxseed per day may provide some health benefits, and is most likely safe," says Lilian Thompson, Ph.D., professor of nutritional sciences at the University of Toronto and one of the leading flaxseed researchers in the world. Dr. Thompson urges certain groups of people (children under 18 years of age; and women who are breast-feeding, pregnant, or trying to conceive) to be cautious about consuming large amounts of flax (3 to 5 tablespoons a day). Breast cancer patients who are taking Tamoxifen should avoid flaxseed as well because researchers don't yet know if lignans will help or adversely interact with that particular drug, according to Dr. Thompson.

What's the Best Way to Store Flax?

Whole flaxseed (not yet ground) can be stored in a dark, dry cabinet for up to a year. But once the flax is ground, it needs to be stored in an airtight, opaque container in the refrigerator (preferably the freezer). Ideally you'll want to use it within two months or so. The omega-3s in flax are sensitive to oxidation, and warm temperatures and light both increase oxidation, which is why storing flax in a dark, cold environment is recommended.

Quick Ways to Get Your Flax

1. **Fruit Is Your Flax Friend.** Sprinkle a tablespoon of ground flaxseed or a scoop of flaxseed-containing cereal (1/4 cup or more) over berries, sliced peaches, or any fresh fruit you enjoy.

2. **Make a Yogurt Parfait.** Make a flaxseed yogurt parfait by topping a serving of your favorite yogurt with some fresh fruit, then top that with a flaxseed–granola mixture. It's so delicious, you won't even notice it's good for you, and you'll be getting a serving of low-fat dairy to boot!

3. **B.Y.O.F.** Bring your own ground flaxseed with you in a resealable plastic bag or plastic food storage container so you can stir it into the smoothies or iced coffee drinks you buy.

4. **Supplement Your Soy Drink With Flax.** Stir a tablespoon or two of ground flaxseed into your favorite soy drink.

5. **Sandwich Flax in Your Sandwich.** Sprinkle a teaspoon or two of ground flaxseed onto the spicy mustard, chutney, cheese spread, peanut butter dressing, or other condiment of choice on your sandwich.

6. **Add Flax to Your Spreads.** Stir 1 1/2 teaspoons of ground flax into a tablespoon of low-sugar jam or preserves (the darker the color, such as raspberry, boysenberry, or blueberry jams, the less noticeable the flax), or a natural-style nut butter, then spread the mixture over a piece of whole grain toast or crackers!

7. **Use Flax in Your Baking.** Bake muffins, bread, or rolls, replacing 1/4 to 1/2 cup of the flour with ground flaxseed if the recipe calls for 2 or more cups of flour.

8. **Use Flax in Your Cooking.** Stir some ground flaxseed into soups, stews, and casseroles. The darker-colored dishes hide flax the best.

9. **Use Flax as a Substitute for Bread Crumbs.** Mix some ground flaxseed into a ground meat mixture like you would bread crumbs when making meat loaf, meatballs, or filling for pasta or tortillas.

Step #6: Is Aspartame Not So Sweet for Your Headaches?

Headache specialists still do not agree on how much of a threat aspartame (a.k.a. NutraSweet and Equal) poses for most migraine sufferers. But the way I see it, this is an easy substance to experimentally cut out. So if you think it might be affecting your headache frequency, give elimination a try. We've included a list of all the aspartame-containing products that we could find in a nearby supermarket in Chapter 6. You will also find a list of the pros and cons of alternative low-cal sweeteners so you can find the best aspartame-free sugar substitute for you.

Step #7: Limit Tyramine-Containing Foods

According to many headache experts, there is abundant evidence to support the thought that vasoactive substances such as tyramine present in foods are, at least in part, responsible for some diet-precipitated vascular headaches.

Tyramine is probably the most difficult food component to figure out where headaches are concerned. Here are the problems as I see it:

- The levels of tyramine can increase significantly in certain foods the longer they are stored, so it is hard to know how much tyramine you are getting in various foods.

- The levels of tyramine can vary with different samples and brands of the same type of food.

- Some of the data on tyramine content of various foods was actually from studies conducted in Europe and Canada decades ago.

The good news is that a recent American study that set out to get some current information on the tyramine content of various suspected foods found that the content of tyramine in "usual portions" of a variety of fresh, non-spoiled foods and beverages commonly consumed in the United States is too small to trigger migraines. But (you knew there would be a "but," didn't you?) there are some foods and beverages that were notably high in tyramine content. It's important to know everything we can about tyramine and what conditions seem to raise tyramine levels in food in case this is a headache trigger for you.

What Is Tyramine?

Tyramine is produced in foods from the natural break-down of the amino acid tyrosine. That's why tyramine levels increase in foods when they are aged, fermented, or stored for long periods of time.

What Is Tyramine's Connection to Headaches and Migraines?

Tyramine has been suspected in the past of being a head-ache trigger for some people. Some experts are currently questioning this connection, however. Meanwhile, many tyramine-rich foods and beverages continue to be named as headache triggers by people across the country.

What Foods Contain Higher Levels of Tyramine?

Older lists of foods that contain high levels of tyramine were based on 30-year-old data from Europe and Canada. So, utilizing recent advances in analytical procedures and taking changes in food manufacturing techniques into account, a group of researchers from the United States reexamined the content of tyramine and phenylethylamine in particular foods a few years back.

This is what they found[6]:

- The beverages they sampled that had tyramine levels greater than 20 micrograms per 12-ounce serving included:
  - Sebastiani Cabernet Sauvignon (around 3,038 µg/ 12 oz.).
  - Cinzano Extra Dry Vermouth (around 2,925 µg/ 12 oz.).

- Miller Lite (around 274 µg/12 oz.).
- Budweiser (around 225 µg/12 oz.).
- Stroh (around 146 µg/12 oz.).

Note: Choose your alcohol wisely, and less is more (keep amounts small).

- For most cheeses they analyzed, after 13 days at 4 °C, there was a small yet significant increase in tyramine. But the levels were much higher in samples stored at 24 °C for 13 days.

The cheeses they sampled that had tyramine levels greater than 10 micrograms per ounce of cheese were:

- Belmont brie, 13 days stored at 24 °C (14 µg/ounce).*
- Blue cheese, fresh from the store (1,047 µg/ounce).
- Cheddar, 113 days at 24 °C (999 µg/ounce).
- Cheddar, 13 days at 4 °C (509 µg/ounce).
- Cheddar, fresh from the store (184 µg/ounce).
- Colby cheese, 13 days at 4 °C (1,782 µg/ounce).
- Colby cheese, 13 days stored at 24 °C (6,395 µg/ounce).
- Colby cheese, fresh from the store (665 to 1,293 µg/ounce).
- Goat cheese, 13 days stored at 24 °C (693 µg/ounce).
- Havarti with dill, fresh from the store or 13 days at 4 °C (around 4,697 µg/ounce).
- Mozzarella, 13 days stored at 24 °C (5,037 µg/ounce).
- French brie samples seemed to contain only small amounts of tyramine, even after being stored for 13 days at 4 °C.

Note: Fresh is best! Buy cheese that is as fresh as possible, and buy your cheese at stores that store their cheese as close to 4 °C as possible. Only buy as much as you need so your cheese isn't sitting in the refrigerator for too long either. Try to choose the types of cheese that tend to have less tyramine. Also, try to find the latest dates on your cheese packages (look toward the back of the display to find the freshest samples). You might consider freezing your cheese between uses, too, if tyramine seems to be a problem for you. Dr. Frederick Freitag of the Diamond Headache Clinic confirmed that Monterey Jack and mozzarella (fresh or low moisture) seem OK to consume in reasonable portions for many headache sufferers.

- Meat samples tended not to have higher levels of tyramine as long as they were stored at 4 °C over 13 days. Being stored at 24 °C did seem to increase tyramine levels, however. Certain types of meat did contain more tyramine than others. Chicken (smoked, sliced, chopped, pressed, or cooked), for example, had a minimum of 5,688 micrograms per ounce when fresh from the store, while turkey had consistently low levels of tyramine when fresh or stored for 13 days at 4 °C. Ground pork had a minimum of 962 micrograms per ounce when fresh from the store, which was similar to the samples of ground sirloin and ground chuck that were fresh from the store. Beef (smoked, sliced, chopped, pressed, or cooked), rather than ground beef, had much lower levels of tyramine (113 micrograms per ounce, fresh from the store).

- Certain seafood samples, such as shrimp, showed dramatic increases in tyramine when stored at 4 °C or 24 °C. Many of the fish samples had less than 10 micrograms per ounce of tyramine when fresh from the store, including scallops, cod, ocean perch, top neck clams, salmon steak, and smoked trout. Other samples contained higher levels. These include:

- Blue point oysters, fresh from the store (52 to 110 µg/ounce).
- Catfish, fresh from the store (18 µg/ounce).
- Gefilte fish, fresh from the store (33 to 291 µg/ounce).
- Mahimahi, fresh from the store (34 to 110 µg/ounce).
- Shark steak, fresh from the store (24 µg/ounce).
- Shrimp, 13 days at 24 °C (4,867 µg/ounce).
- Shrimp, fresh from the store (31 µg/ounce).
- Shrimp, two days stored at 4 °C (1,358 µg/ounce).
- Smoked Alaskan salmon, fresh from the store (around 31 µg/ounce).
- Smoked Great Lakes whitefish, fresh from the store (around 560 µg/ounce).
- Sole, fresh from the store (around 17 to 34 µg/ounce).
- Tilapia, skinless, fresh from the store (90 to 435 µg/ounce).
- Walleyed pike, fresh from the store (302 to 492 µg/ounce).

- Most of the beans (black beans, pink beans, red kidney beans, small white beans, and chick peas) they sampled were very low in tyramine, with less than 1 microgram per 1/4 cup.

- Some suspected trouble foods, such as olives, sauerkraut, and chocolate, were also tested. Olives contained less than 1 microgram per ounce, and sauerkraut and chocolate only ran up about 3 micrograms per ounce.

F.Y.I. Hold the Cheese (and Some Dairy), Please!

Looking at the lists of cheeses to avoid given out by many headache clinics, one wonders . . . what cheeses are left?

Cheeses You Can Use

Ripened cheeses are on several "avoid" lists from various headache clinics and foundations. There are so many cheeses listed to avoid that it is easier to list the cheeses that may not cause you problems. They are:

- Cottage cheese.
- Cream cheese.
- Monterey Jack (thought to be OK for many).
- Mozzarella, fresh or low moisture (thought to be OK for many).
- Ricotta.

What About Other Dairy Products?

One other dairy product listed as being potentially problematic is sour cream. Some experts advise to limit your intake of sour cream to only 1/2 cup per day.

Step #8: Avoid Certain Additives

Headache specialists still do not agree on how much of a threat MSG and nitrates/nitrites pose for most migraine sufferers. Some headache researchers think there is a connection, and that nitrates/nitrites, for example, possibly dilate blood vessels, which may then cause headaches in some people. If you find after filling out your headache diary that you are sensitive to MSG and/or nitrates/nitrites, you can check out the lists of products that contain these two additives in Chapter 6. By avoiding these products and choosing alternatives that do not contain MSG or nitrates/nitrites, you'll be able to see if your headaches improve!

Step #9: Beware of Certain Dehydrating Beverages, and Keep Hydrated

Dehydration can trigger headaches, so try to keep yourself hydrated by drinking plenty of good ol' H_2O and limiting your consumption of beverages that tend to deplete your body's water reserves, such as alcohol and caffeine-containing drinks.

Drinking fluids that promote good hydration keeps a more constant blood volume in your body, which reduces the likelihood of headaches triggered by dehydration. Makes sense, doesn't it?

Better Beverages to Try Instead

- Mineral water with subtle flavors, but no calories (Calistoga, Crystal Geyser, and Perrier, for example).
- Water with ice and a twist of lemon or lime.
- Decaf herbal teas (cold or hot).
- Decaf coffee.
- 100% fruit juice (avoid citrus juices if citrus is a headache trigger for you).
- Nonalcoholic beer.
- Nonfat or 1% milk.

Step #10: Work Magnesium-Rich Foods Into Your Diet

Magnesium is one of the minerals that continue to exist under the nutritional radar of most books and articles, but it is actually quite important in its own right. The fact that it can help people who suffer from hormonal headaches is just one more nutritional notch on its belt.

More on Magnesium

The recommended daily intake for magnesium is 320 milligrams per day for women 31 years and older, and 420 milligrams per day for men 31 years and older.

Magnesium has a variety of functions in the human body, so it's no surprise that you can find it throughout the body. About 50 percent of the body's magnesium works with calcium and phosphorus to make and maintain strong bones, while 40 percent is in the muscles and soft tissues (muscle contraction and the conduction of nerve impulses require magnesium). But that's only the beginning. Adequate magnesium, working together with calcium, can help lower blood pressure and discourage osteoporosis. There also seems to be an association between low-magnesium diets and the promotion of atherosclerosis (fatty deposits in the artery walls).

Top Magnesium-Rich Foods

Generally you'll find magnesium in all sorts of good-for-you foods, such as whole grains, nuts, seeds, soybeans, tofu, dark-green vegetables, beans, fish, and yogurt. So by just eating healthier foods, you will naturally get more magnesium. To give you some specific foods to try to work into your diet, here is my list of the top magnesium-rich foods:

Magnesium-Rich Foods	
Food Item (100 g)	**Magnesium (mg)**
Almonds, roasted	286
Almonds, slivered	304
Bagel, whole grain	141
Barley, dry	133
Black beans, dry	171
Black-eyed peas (cowpeas), raw	184
Bran cereal with raisins	150
Brazil nuts	225
Bread, 100% whole grain	118
Brown rice, dry	143
Buckwheat flour, whole	251
Bulgur, dry	164
Cashews, roasted	260
Chex, Multi-Bran	122
Chex, Wheat	112
Chocolate chips, semisweet	115
Cornmeal, whole grain	127
Cornnuts	113
Fish roe	300
Flaxseed, ground	362
Flour, whole wheat	138
Garbanzo beans, dry	115
Granola bar, peanut	110
Granola cereal, homemade with oats and wheat germ	178

Magnesium-Rich Foods (cont.)	
Food Item (100 g)	**Magnesium (mg)**
Great Northern beans, dry	189
Halibut, baked	107
Halibut, smoked	136
Hazelnuts, roasted	173
Instant oatmeal, dry packet	148
Kasha, roasted, dry	221
Lima beans, dry	224
Macadamia nuts	130
Matzoh, whole wheat	134
Milk, nonfat, dry	162
Millet, dry	114
Mixed nuts, roasted	235
Molasses	242
Navy beans, boiled	111
Oat bran muffin	157
Oat bran, dry	235
Old-fashioned oats	270
Peanut butter, chunky	159
Peanuts, roasted	188
Pecans, roasted	132
Pine nuts, dried	233
Pink beans, dry	182
Pistachio nuts	121
Popcorn, air-popped	131
Post 100% Bran	278

Magnesium-Rich Foods (cont.)

Food Item (100 g)	Magnesium (mg)
Post Bran Flakes	214
Pumpkin seeds, roasted	534
Quaker Breakfast Squares	125
Quinoa, dry	210
Red kidney beans, raw	138
Roman Meal, dry	237
Rye bread	187
Rye, whole grain	121
Salmon fillet, broiled	122
Shredded wheat cereal	170
Soy flour, defatted version	290
Soy flour, regular	369
Soybeans, raw	280
Sundried tomatoes	194
Sunflower seeds, raw	353
Sunflower seeds, roasted	129
Tahini (sesame butter)	353
Walnuts	202
Wheat, whole grain, dry	126
Wheat bran	611
Wheat germ, raw	239
Wheaties	106
White beans, dry	190

F.Y.I. Other Foods You Might Want to Watch Out For

Just in case, here are a few other foods that some research has pointed the finger at as being possible headache triggers.

Histamine-Rich Foods

Some studies have shown that histamine-rich foods cause a worsening of symptoms in patients suffering from chronic headaches.[7]

Histamine-rich foods include:

- Alcoholic beverages.
- Cheese.
- Fish.
- Hard cured sausages.
- Pickled cabbage.

Elimination and Reintroduction

One study found that the following foods were recognized as being responsible for migraine attacks in 12 migraine sufferers, ages 7 to 18, after an elimination and reintroduction diet:[8]

- Bananas.
- Cacao (cocoa and chocolate).
- Eggs.
- Hazelnuts.

Comparison of Diet and Headaches

One Italian study found the percentage of people sensitive to particular foods was similar for both migraine

⇨

and tension-type headache sufferers. These were the most common headache triggers:[9]

- Alcoholic drinks.
- Cheese.
- Chocolate.

Possible Food Allergens Associated With Migraines

Spanish researchers believe some foods can spark migraine attacks in susceptible people.[10] They cite the following foods as possibly bringing on a migraine attack:

- Alcoholic drinks (red wine, beer, and whisky distilled in copper stills).
- Bananas.
- Beans.
- Cereals.
- Cheese.
- Chocolate.
- Citrus fruits.
- Coffee.
- Cola drinks.
- Cured meats.
- Dairy products.
- Food additives (nitrates/nitrites, MSG, and aspartame).
- Hot dogs.
- Nuts.
- Pizza.
- Tea.

Chapter 5

21 Recipes That May Help Your Headaches

H
ere you will find some healthy alternatives to dishes that have been identified as potential headache triggers. I've included some basics, including two recipes for homemade broth, plus a recipe for homemade vegetable gravy—all of which you can substitute in any of your favorite recipes. There are some recipes using navy beans, a bean that has been credited with being tolerated well by headache sufferers. You will also find ricotta and cottage cheese used as an alternative to potentially problematic cheeses. I threw in a few fun turkey recipes, too, because turkey seems to be a meat impressively low in tyramine.

Brunch

Mini Spinach Frittatas

These make a nice presentation when served with a garnish of fresh salsa on top and a sprig or two of fresh cilantro.

Makes 6 servings (2 mini frittatas each, the size of cupcakes)

- 2 large eggs (omega-3 enriched, if available)
- 1/2 cup egg substitute (regular or flavored)
- 1/4 cup fat-free half-and-half
- 1/4 tsp. hot sauce
- 1 tsp. lemon pepper
- 1 1/2 tsp. parsley flakes (or 1 tbs. freshly chopped parsley)
- 2/3 cup frozen chopped spinach, thawed and gently squeezed of excess water
- 1 cup part-skim ricotta
- 2 tbs. fat-free sour cream
- 1/4 cup shredded Parmesan cheese (omit this if you can't tolerate 2 tsp. of Parmesan per serving)
- 6 tbs. fresh salsa

1. Preheat oven to 375 °F. Coat a 12-cup muffin tin with canola cooking spray.
2. In a large mixing bowl, beat the eggs, egg substitute, fat-free half-and-half, hot sauce, lemon pepper, and parsley together on medium speed until well blended.
3. Add the spinach, ricotta, sour cream, and Parmesan cheese to the mixing bowl and beat on medium-low speed until everything is nicely blended.
4. Spoon frittata mixture using a 1/4-cup scoop into the muffin tin and bake for 20 to 25 minutes. Let stand for five minutes, then remove from the muffin cups. Garnish the top of each mini frittata with about 1/2 Tbs. of salsa, and serve!

Per serving: 126 calories; 12 g protein; 6.2 g carbohydrate; 6 g fat (3.2 g saturated fat, 1.9 g monounsaturated fat, .4 g polyunsaturated fat); 87 mg cholesterol; 1 g fiber; 207 mg sodium; 25 mg magnesium; .1 g tryptophan; .4 g tyrosine; .1 g omega-3 fatty acids; .3 g omega-6 fatty acids. Calories from fat: 42 percent.

 ## Irish Egg Skillet

Makes 2 servings

- 2 medium potatoes
- 2 large eggs (omega-3 enriched, if available)
- 1/2 cup egg substitute
- 1 tbs. canola oil
- 1/2 cup finely chopped onion
- 1/2 cup finely chopped bell pepper, red or green
- Pepper to taste
- Salt to taste (optional)
- 2 tbs. green part of green onions (or 1 tbs. chopped chives)

1. Use microwave to cook potatoes until tender (make sure to pierce each potato a couple of times with a fork to help the potatoes vent as they cook). Let cool (they can cool overnight in the refrigerator).

2. Cut potatoes into 1/4-inch slices. Whisk the eggs and the egg substitute together until well blended, and put aside.

3. Start heating a large nonstick skillet or frying pan over medium-high heat. Coat the bottom of the pan with canola oil and add potatoes, onion, and pepper. Sauté the vegetables, gently flipping them over and stirring occasionally until potatoes are nicely browned (about 6 minutes). Add pepper to taste (and salt to taste, if desired).

4. Pour in the egg mixture and gently stir everything around a little. Sprinkle green onions or chives over the top, and cover the frying pan or skillet. Cook on medium heat until eggs are set (about 4 minutes). Serve with ketchup, if desired!

Per serving: 490 calories; 20 g protein; 76 g carbohydrate; 12 g fat (2.2 g saturated fat, 6.1 g monounsaturated fat, 3 g polyunsaturated fat); 212 mg cholesterol; 9 g fiber; 213 mg sodium; 88 mg magnesium; .2 g tryptophan; .5 g tyrosine; .7 g omega-3 fatty acids; 2.2 g omega-6 fatty acids. Calories from fat: 22 percent.

 Fresh Fruit Muffins

These muffins are lower in fat and higher in fiber than typical muffins. To keep them free of headache triggers and to add some flavor and color, we are using fresh fruit instead of dried fruit. Use whatever non-citrus fresh fruit you desire, such as raspberries, blueberries, chopped peaches, or cranberries. The topping adds a fun look and taste, but if you want to cut to the quick, just omit it!

Makes 9 muffins

- 3/4 cup whole wheat flour
- 3/4 cup white flour
- 1/4 cup non-aspartame sugar substitute, such as Splenda (if you don't want to use a sugar substitute, just use 1/2 cup sugar instead)
- 1/2 cup sugar
- 1/2 tsp. salt
- 2 tsp. baking powder
- 3 tbs. canola oil
- 1 large egg
- 9 tbs. fat-free half-and-half
- 1 1/4 cup non-trigger fresh or frozen fruit (blueberries, cranberries, or chopped peaches, for example)

Topping
- 1/3 cup white sugar
- 1/3 cup white flour
- 1 1/2 tsp. ground cinnamon
- 2 tbs. no-trans or low-trans margarine (no more than 8 g fat/tbs.; Land O'Lakes Fresh Buttery Taste Spread, for example)
- 1 tsp. fat-free half-and-half

1. Preheat oven to 400 °F. Line muffin pan with muffin liners.
2. Add the whole wheat flour, white flour, sugar substitute, sugar, salt, and baking powder to a large mixing bowl and beat on low to combine.
3. Add canola oil, egg, and fat-free half-and-half to the dry mixture. Beat on low until combined.
4. Fold in your fruit of choice. Divide the batter evenly into the muffin tin.
5. To make crumb topping, add white sugar, white flour, and cinnamon to a small food processor bowl and pulse briefly to blend. Add margarine and fat-free half-and-half. Pulse briefly until a crumb mixture forms. (If you don't have a small food processor, blend mixture together with a fork.)
6. Sprinkle crumb topping evenly over the muffins and bake for 20 to 25 minutes, or until done.

Per muffin (with topping): 232 calories; 5.5 g protein; 38 g carbohydrate; 7 g fat (.8 g saturated fat, 3.5 g monounsaturated fat, 2 g polyunsaturated fat); 24 mg cholesterol; 2.5 g fiber; 289 mg sodium; 10 mg magnesium; .04 g tryptophan; .13 g tyrosine; .5 g omega-3 fatty acids; 1.1 g omega-6 fatty acids. Calories from fat: 27 percent.

Per muffin (without topping): 177 calories; 5 g protein; 27 g carbohydrate; 5.5 g fat (.6 g saturated fat, 3 g monounsaturated fat, 1.5 g polyunsaturated fat); 24 mg cholesterol;

2.2 g fiber; 264 mg sodium; 9 mg magnesium; .04 g tryptophan; .12 g tyrosine; 1 g omega-3 fatty acids; 1 g omega-6
fatty acids. Calories from fat: 28 percent.

 ## Wheat Drop Biscuits

These biscuits are extra easy to make because we are
using a food processor to cut in the margarine, and then
we are dropping the dough onto the cookie sheet instead
of cutting into biscuits.

Makes 12 biscuits

- 1 cup whole wheat flour
- 1 cup unbleached white flour
- 1 tbs. baking powder
- 1/2 tsp. salt
- 1/4 cup no-trans margarine, frozen (no more
  than 8 g fat/tbs.; Take Control, for example)
- 1 cup fat-free half-and-half (or low-fat milk)

1. Preheat oven to 450 °F. Coat a baking sheet
   with canola cooking spray.

2. Add whole wheat flour, white flour, baking
   powder, and salt to a large food processor bowl
   and pulse to blend.

3. Add frozen margarine in small chunks to the
   food processor bowl. Pulse to blend with flour
   mixture.

4. Pour fat-free half-and-half into the food
   processor bowl. Briefly pulse until dough is
   formed.

5. Drop dough by heaping tablespoons onto
   prepared baking sheet, and bake until golden
   brown (about 12 to 15 minutes).

Per biscuit: 126 calories; 4.5 g protein; 19 g carbohydrate; 3 g fat (.4 g saturated fat, 1.5 g monounsaturated fat, .7 g polyunsaturated fat); 1 mg cholesterol; 1.3 g fiber; 149 mg sodium; 6 mg magnesium; .02 g tryptophan; .07 g tyrosine; .2 g omega-3 fatty acids; .4 g omega-6 fatty acids. Calories from fat: 21 percent.

Tuna and Bean Salad

Makes 4 servings

- 1 1/2 cups cut green beans, frozen
- 6 oz. albacore tuna canned in water, drained
- 3/4 cup canned navy beans, drained and rinsed
- 1/2 cup finely chopped red onion
- 1 1/2 tbs. olive oil
- 2 tbs. lemon juice (if citrus is a trigger for you, use apple juice or other fruit juice)
- 2 tsp. minced garlic
- 1 tsp. dill weed
- Freshly ground pepper to taste
- Salt to taste (optional)

1. Add green beans, tuna, navy beans, red onion, olive oil, lemon juice, garlic, and dill weed to a medium serving bowl. Toss well.
2. Add black pepper to taste (and salt to taste, if desired). Cover and chill in refrigerator for about two hours. Enjoy with whole grain crackers if desired.

Per serving: 189 calories; 15 g protein; 17 g carbohydrate; 6.5 g fat (1.2 g saturated fat, 4.3 g monounsaturated fat, 1 g polyunsaturated fat); 18 mg cholesterol; 4.5 g fiber; 385 mg sodium; 53 mg magnesium; .2 g tryptophan; .45 g tyrosine; .5 g omega-3 fatty acids; .5 g omega-6 fatty acids. Calories from fat: 31 percent.

Dinner Entrees

Jumbo Shells With Marinara

Makes about 7 servings (2 shells each)

- 15 jumbo shells (about 5 1/2 oz. dry)
- 15 oz. part-skim ricotta
- 10-oz. box frozen chopped spinach, thawed and squeezed of excess water
- 4 green onions (white and part of green), finely chopped
- 1/2 to 1 tsp. garlic powder (depending on preference)
- 1/2 to 1 tsp. dried oregano leaves (depending on preference)
- 1/2 tsp. black pepper
- 26-oz. jar marinara

1. Preheat oven to 400 °F. Coat a 9 × 13-inch (or similar) baking dish with canola cooking spray.
2. Bring a large saucepan of water to a full boil and add the pasta shells. Lower heat to maintain a gentle boil. Boil until tender, according to package directions. Drain and rinse with cold water.
3. In a medium-size bowl, blend ricotta with spinach, green onions, garlic powder, oregano, and black pepper. Fill the pasta shells evenly with the ricotta filling and place in the prepared pan (open side of pasta shells face-up). Drizzle marinara sauce evenly over the shells. Cover with foil and bake in the oven for about 25 minutes.

Per serving: 141 calories; 9 g protein; 15.5 g carbohydrate; 5.5 g fat (3 g saturated fat, 1.4 g monounsaturated fat, .2 g polyunsaturated fat); 19 mg cholesterol; 3.2 g fiber; 450 mg sodium; 34 mg magnesium; .1 g tryptophan; .36 g tyrosine; .1 g omega-3 fatty acids; .1 g omega-6 fatty acids. Calories from fat: 35 percent.

Cheesy Turkey or Chicken Enchiladas

You will be surprised how well the cottage cheese mixture works with the turkey or chicken to make a great-tasting enchilada.

Makes 10 enchiladas

- 2 tsp. canola oil
- 2/3 cup chopped sweet or yellow onion
- 3 cups roasted turkey or chicken breast, shredded (boneless and skinless)
- 7-oz. can green chili peppers, chopped (including the juice)
- 2 tbs. taco seasoning, low-sodium
- 1/3 cup water
- 1/2 cup fat-free sour cream
- 2 cups small curd cottage cheese
- 1/2 tsp. salt
- 1/4 to 1/2 tsp. freshly ground pepper (depending on preference)
- 10 6-inch corn tortillas
- 1 cup shredded reduced-fat Monterey Jack or soy cheese (optional)
- 17.25-oz. bottle enchilada sauce

1. Preheat oven to 350 °F. Coat a 9 × 13-inch baking dish with canola cooking spray.

2.   Heat canola oil in nonstick medium saucepan over medium-high heat. Add onions and sauté for a few minutes. Add turkey or chicken, green chili peppers (including juice), taco seasoning, and water to the onions. Simmer together for three to five minutes to blend flavors.

3.   In a medium bowl, blend the sour cream, cottage cheese, salt, and pepper together well. Wrap tortillas in a somewhat damp kitchen towel and microwave on high for about two minutes, or until tortillas are nice and soft.

4.   To assemble, sprinkle a rounded tablespoon of Monterey Jack cheese down the center of a tortilla, if desired. Top that with a scant 1/4 cup of the cottage cheese mixture. Place a slightly rounded 1/4 cup of the chicken mixture on top that. Roll up the tortilla to make an enchilada. Place in the prepared pan, seam-side down. Assemble the other nine enchiladas and place in pan. Spread enchilada sauce evenly over the top.

5.   Bake for about 30 minutes or until cheese is melted and bubbly.

Per enchilada (with chicken and Monterey Jack): 259 calories; 24 g protein; 23 g carbohydrate; 8 g fat (2.9 g saturated fat, 1.3 g monounsaturated fat, .9 g polyunsaturated fat); 51 mg cholesterol; 2.1 g fiber; 790 mg sodium; 32 mg magnesium; .17 g tryptophan; .51 g tyrosine; .2 g omega-3 fatty acids; .7 g omega-6 fatty acids. Calories from fat: 28 percent.

Per enchilada (with chicken and without Monterey Jack): 226 calories; 21 g protein; 23 g carbohydrate; 5.5 g fat (1.3 g saturated fat, 1.3 g monounsaturated fat, .9 g polyunsaturated fat); 43 mg cholesterol; 2.1 g fiber; 690 mg sodium; 32 mg magnesium; .17 g tryptophan; .51 g tyrosine; .2 g omega-3 fatty acids; .7 g omega-6 fatty acids. Calories from fat: 22 percent.

Low-Fat Chicken Broth

This recipe is actually pretty easy to throw together. Afterwards you not only have 6 cups of broth, you also have about 3 cups of cooked chicken once you shred it off the bones.

Makes about 6 cups of broth

- 2 chicken breasts with bone (skinless)
- 2 chicken thighs with bone (skinless)
- 1 large onion, quartered
- 3 stalks celery, including some leaves, cut into 1-inch chunks
- 1 large carrot, cut into 1-inch chunks
- 1/2 tsp. salt
- 3 whole cloves
- 6 cups water

1. Add chicken pieces, onion, celery, carrot, salt, and cloves to a large saucepan or soup pot. Add water and bring to a boil. Reduce heat, cover, and simmer for one hour.

2. Remove chicken pieces and vegetable chunks, then strain the broth.

3. Keep the broth covered in the refrigerator until needed. Freeze some portions of it if you aren't using all of the broth within a few days.

Per cup: 16 calories; 1 g protein; 2 g carbohydrate; .3 g fat (0 g saturated fat, .1 g monounsaturated fat, .2 g polyunsaturated fat); 5 mg cholesterol; 1 g fiber; 198 mg sodium; 0 g magnesium; 0 g tryptophan; 0 g tyrosine; 0 g omega-3 fatty acids; 0 g omega-6 fatty acids. Calories from fat: 17 percent.

 ## Vegetarian Broth

This is a basic vegetable broth recipe. You can add your own touch by adding or substituting any herbs you like or by adding or substituting any vegetables you prefer. You can use the vegetables you strain out as an ingredient for stews and casseroles, for example, or you can just discard them.

Makes about 8 cups of broth

- 1 tbs. canola or olive oil
- 1 large onion, cut into 1-inch chunks
- 2 stalks celery, including some leaves, cut into 1-inch chunks
- 2 large carrots, cut into 1-inch chunks
- 1 1/2 tbs. minced garlic
- 8 sprigs fresh parsley
- 6 sprigs fresh thyme
- 2 bay leaves
- 1/2 tsp. salt
- 8 cups water

1. Heat oil in large nonstick saucepan or soup pot. Add onion, celery, carrots, garlic, parsley, thyme, and bay leaves, then stir. Cook over high heat for about five minutes, stirring frequently.

2. Add salt and water, and bring to a boil. Lower heat to simmer, and cook uncovered for 30 minutes. Strain the broth mixture.

3. Keep the broth covered and in the refrigerator until needed. Freeze some portions of it if you aren't using all of the broth within a few days.

Per cup: 30 calories; 1 g protein; 5 g carbohydrate; .5 g fat (0 g saturated fat, .1 g monounsaturated fat, .4 g polyunsaturated

fat); 0 mg cholesterol; 1 g fiber; 148 mg sodium; 0 g magnesium; 0 g tryptophan; 0 g tyrosine; 0 g omega-3 fatty acids;
0 g omega-6 fatty acids. Calories from fat: 15 percent.

Savory Vegetable Gravy

Makes 2 cups of gravy

- 1/4 pound (about 1 1/2 cups) fresh cremini mushroom slices
- 1/2 cup onion, finely chopped
- 2 tbs. no-trans margarine (no more than 8 g fat/Tbs.)
- 1 cup low-sodium vegetable broth
- 2 tsp. finely chopped fresh parsley (or 1 tsp. parsley flakes)
- 1/4 tsp. celery salt
- 1/2 tsp. freshly ground pepper
- 2 tbs. quick-mixing all-purpose flour (Wondra, for example)
- 1 cup fat-free half-and-half, divided use (low-fat milk or plain soymilk can be substituted)

1. In a medium nonstick saucepan, brown mushroom slices and onion in margarine over medium-high heat. Add broth, parsley, celery salt, and pepper. Reduce heat and simmer for a few minutes.
2. In a 4-cup measure, whisk flour with 4 tbs. fat-free half-and-half until smooth. Whisk in the remaining half-and-half, and then pour into the vegetable mixture. Simmer until thickened, stirring frequently.

Per 1/4 cup: 68 calories; 4 g protein; 7 g carbohydrate; 2.9 g fat (.4 g saturated fat, 1.4 g monounsaturated fat, .8 g polyunsaturated fat); 0 mg cholesterol; 1 g fiber; 113 mg sodium; 11 mg magnesium; .04 g tryptophan; 0 g tyrosine; 0 g omega-3 fatty acids; 0 g omega-6 fatty acids. Calories from fat: 38 percent.

 ## Turkey and Cranberry Sandwich

Turkey is one of the meats with the lowest levels of tyramine, and here is one of my favorite turkey sandwich recipes.

Makes 1 sandwich

- 2 slices whole grain bread (or 1 whole grain roll)
- 1 to 2 tbs. light cream cheese
- 1 to 2 tbs. cranberry sauce
- A couple of carved slices of turkey (about the size of the palm of your hand)
- Lettuce, tomato, sliced onion, and alfalfa sprouts (as desired)

1. Spread the cream cheese over one of the slices of bread. Spread cranberry sauce over that.
2. Add the slices of turkey and top with lettuce, tomato, sliced onion, and alfalfa sprouts, as desired. Enjoy!

Per sandwich (using 2 oz. of turkey and 1.5 tbs. of both cream cheese and cranberry sauce): 317 calories; 24 g protein; 36 g carbohydrate; 8.5 g fat (3 g saturated fat, 2.6 g monounsaturated fat, 1.7 g polyunsaturated fat); 50 mg cholesterol; 4 g fiber; 415 mg sodium; 63 mg magnesium; .3 g tryptophan; 0 g tyrosine; .1 g omega-3 fatty acids; 1.5 g omega-6 fatty acids. Calories from fat: 24 percent.

The Day-After Irish Shepherd's Pie

This is a wonderful way to enjoy leftover mashed potatoes, green vegetables, and gravy!

Makes 6 servings

- 2/3 cup chopped mild or sweet onion
- 2 cups diced roasted turkey
- 2 cups leftover homemade gravy (the Savory Vegetable Gravy on page 131 works great)
- 1/2 to 1 tsp. Worcestershire sauce (optional)
- 1 to 2 cups assorted leftover vegetables (chopped carrots, green beans, or broccoli, for example)
- 2 cups leftover mashed potatoes
- 1 tbs. butter (or no- or low-trans margarine)
- Freshly ground black pepper (optional)

1. Preheat the oven to 400 °F. Coat the inside of a deep-dish pie plate with canola cooking spray.

2. Coat a large nonstick skillet with canola cooking spray. Add the onion, and cook until lightly browned. With a spatula, stir in the diced turkey, gravy, Worcestershire sauce (if desired), and vegetables.

3. Spread the turkey mixture evenly in the prepared pie plate. Spread the mashed potatoes evenly over the mixture. With a fork, make a design in the mashed potatoes. Set aside.

4. Melt the butter in a microwave-safe cup, or melt it in a saucepan over low heat on the stove. With a pastry brush, brush the top of the potatoes with the melted butter. (Sprinkle black pepper over the top, if desired.)

5. Place pie dish in the oven and cook until heated through and golden on top (about 25 minutes).

Per serving: 247 calories; 20 g protein; 27 g carbohydrate; 7.5 g fat (1.8 g saturated fat, 3 g monounsaturated fat, 2 g polyunsaturated fat); 38 mg cholesterol; 4.5 g fiber; 380 mg sodium; 38 mg magnesium; .3 g tryptophan; 0 g tyrosine; .2 g omega-3 fatty acids; .9 g omega-6 fatty acids. Calories from fat: 27 percent.

 ## Turkey Fettuccini Alfredo

You will love this totally creamy and comforting dish.

Makes 4 servings

- 1/4 cup light cream cheese
- 1 1/2 cups fat-free half-and-half or whole milk, divided use
- 1 tbs. quick-mixing all-purpose flour (Wondra, for example)
- 1 tbs. butter (or no- or low-trans margarine)
- 3 cups hot spaghetti or fettuccine (whole wheat if desired), cooked and drained
- 2 1/2 cups roasted turkey breast, cut into strips (skinless)
- Salt and freshly grated pepper to taste
- Pinch or two of nutmeg (add more to taste, if desired)
- 1/2 cup reduced-fat Monterey Jack, shredded
- 2 to 4 tbs. shredded Parmesan cheese (optional and depending on tolerance)

1. Prepare noodles according to package directions if you haven't already.
2. Combine cream cheese, 1/4 cup of fat-free half-and-half, and flour in a small mixing bowl or food processor. Beat or pulse until well blended. Slowly pour in remaining half-and-half and beat until smooth.

3. Melt 1 tbs. butter in a large nonstick frying pan or saucepan over medium heat. Add the half-and-half mixture and continue to heat, stirring constantly, until the sauce is just the right thickness (about three to four minutes). Turn the heat to low and add the hot noodles and turkey strips. Toss to coat noodles and turkey well with sauce. Add salt and pepper (and nutmeg, if desired). Stir in grated Monterey Jack cheese (and Parmesan, if desired), and serve.

Per serving: 454 calories; 38 g protein; 43 g carbohydrate; 13 g fat (6.4 g saturated fat, 3 g monounsaturated fat, 1.8 g polyunsaturated fat); 80 mg cholesterol; 2 g fiber; 357 mg sodium; 64 mg magnesium; .4 g tryptophan; 0 g tyrosine; .2 g omega-3 fatty acids; 1.6 g omega-6 fatty acids. Calories from fat: 26 percent.

Note: Using whole wheat pasta will increase the fiber to 5 g per serving and the magnesium from 63 mg to 76 mg per serving!

Turkey Navy Bean Chili

Now you can have your chili and eat it, too! This chili uses navy beans (which are an allowed bean), as well as home spices instead of a commercial chili spice packet or canned chili.

Makes about 8 servings

- 1 tbs. canola oil
- 1 cup chopped onion
- 2 tsp. minced garlic
- 2 cups homemade chicken broth (or vegetable broth)
- 18.75-oz. can tomatillos, drained and chopped
- 16-oz. can diced tomatoes

- 7-oz. can diced green chilies
- 1/2 tsp. dried oregano
- 1/2 cup ground coriander seed
- 1/4 tsp. ground cumin
- 1 lb. extra-lean ground turkey, 94% fat free (or ground sirloin)
- 15-oz. can navy beans, drained and rinsed
- 1 cup fresh or frozen corn kernels
- Ground black pepper to taste
- Salt to taste (optional)

1. Heat oil in a large nonstick saucepan over medium-high heat. Add onion and garlic. Sauté until soft (about four minutes).
2. Stir broth, tomatillos, tomatoes, chilies, oregano, coriander, and cumin into the large saucepan with the onion mixture. Bring mixture to a boil, then cover and simmer about 10 minutes.
3. Meanwhile, heat a large nonstick frying pan or skillet over medium-high heat. Coat with canola cooking spray and add a pound of ground turkey. Use a potato masher to break the meat into smaller chunks as it cooks. Continue to cook, using the potato masher to break up the meat, until it is thoroughly cooked and nicely browned. Set aside.
4. After the tomato mixture has simmered for 10 minutes, stir in the navy beans, corn, and meat. Cover the saucepan and simmer for about 5 minutes. Season with pepper to taste (and salt to taste, if desired).
5. Serve each cup of chili with a dollop of fat-free sour cream and baked or reduced-fat tortilla chips on the side, if desired.

Per serving: 157 calories; 8 g protein; 27 g carbohydrate; 3 g fat (.3 g saturated fat, 1.2 g monounsaturated fat, 1 g polyunsaturated fat); 1 mg cholesterol; 7 g fiber; 567 mg sodium; 46 mg magnesium; .06 g tryptophan; .15 g tyrosine; .2 g omega-3 fatty acids; .7 g omega-6 fatty acids. Calories from fat: 17 percent.

Creamy Turkey or Chicken Spinach Lasagna

If chicken seems to be a trigger for you, make sure to use turkey for this recipe. Find a rotisserie restaurant or deli in your neighborhood that sells fresh-roasted sliced turkey, and this recipe will be even easier to make.

Makes 12 servings

- 9 lasagna noodles (about 9 oz. dry)
- 1/4 cup no-trans margarine (no more than 8 g fat/tbs.)
- 1 cup chopped onion
- 2 tsp. minced garlic
- 1/2 cup quick-mixing all-purpose flour, such as Wondra (or unbleached white flour)
- 1/2 tsp. salt
- 2 cups fat-free half-and-half, divided (or low-fat milk)
- 2 cups homemade chicken broth
- 2 cups reduced-fat Monterey Jack, shredded (or soy cheese)
- 2 tsp. Italian seasoning
- 1/2 tsp. ground black pepper
- 2 cups part-skim ricotta
- 3 cups roasted turkey or chicken breast, shredded or cubed (skinless and boneless)
- 2 10-oz. boxes frozen chopped spinach, thawed and gently squeezed of excess of water

1.   Preheat oven to 350 °F. Bring a large pot of lightly salted water to a boil. Add lasagna noodles and boil for eight to 10 minutes. Drain and rinse with cold water.

2.   Melt the margarine in a large nonstick saucepan over medium heat. Add onion and garlic. Cook, stirring frequently, until onions are tender. Whisk in the flour, salt, and 1/2 cup of fat-free half-and-half. Simmer until bubbly. Whisk in the broth and the remaining half-and-half. Boil, stirring constantly, for one minute. Stir in the shredded cheese, Italian seasoning, and pepper. Remove from heat and set aside.

3.   Spread 1/3 cup of the white sauce in the bottom of a 9 × 13-inch baking dish. Layer with three of the noodles, the ricotta, and the turkey or chicken.

4.   Top with three more noodles. Top that layer with 1/3 cup of the white sauce and the spinach. Arrange the last three noodles on top, and spread the remaining white sauce over them.

5.   Bake uncovered in oven for 40 minutes, or until sauce is hot and bubbling. Enjoy!

Per serving: 338 calories; 29 g protein; 31 g carbohydrate; 11 g fat (5.5 g saturated fat, 1.4 g monounsaturated fat, .4 g polyunsaturated fat); 58 mg cholesterol; 3 g fiber; 580 mg sodium; 42 mg magnesium; .22 g tryptophan; .74 g tyrosine; .1 g omega-3 fatty acids; .3 g omega-6 fatty acids. Calories from fat: 29 percent.

Tuna Casserole

This recipe doesn't use the standard cream of mushroom soup. Instead, we will make our own sauce, free of headache triggers. Also, use whatever cheese you can best handle.

We are only using a little bit of sour cream in this recipe, but if even a little bit of sour cream seems to trigger your headaches, drop the sour cream completely and increase the light or low-fat mayonnaise to 3/4 cup.

Makes 6 servings

- 6 cups cooked egg noodles or fettuccine noodles (about 9 oz. fresh)
- 2 6-oz. cans solid white tuna canned in water, drained and broken into small chunks with a fork
- 1 cup celery, chopped
- 1/2 cup green onions, chopped
- 1/2 cup green soybeans or petite peas (only if this isn't a trigger for you)
- 1/2 cup + 2 tbs. fat-free sour cream
- 2 tsp. prepared mustard
- 1/4 cup light mayonnaise
- 1 cup reduced-fat Monterey Jack, shredded (or thinly sliced farmers cheese, fresh mozzarella, or cheddar soy cheese)
- 1/2 tsp. dried thyme
- 1/4 tsp. salt (optional)
- 1 large tomato, chopped

1. Preheat oven to 350 °F. Coat a 2-quart casserole dish or similar baking dish with canola cooking spray.
2. In a large mixing bowl, toss together the cooked noodles, tuna, celery, green onion, and soybeans or peas. Stir in the sour cream, mustard, light mayonnaise, and half of the cheese. Season with thyme and salt (if desired).
3. Spoon the mixture into the prepared casserole dish. Sprinkle or dot the top with the remaining cheese.

4. Bake in the oven for 30 minutes, until hot and bubbly. Sprinkle tomatoes over the top before dishing it up.

Per serving: 410 calories; 30 g protein; 50 g carbohydrate; 12 g fat (4.5 g saturated fat, 2 g monounsaturated fat, 2.4 g polyunsaturated fat); 96 mg cholesterol; 4 g fiber; 520 mg sodium; 70 mg magnesium; .3 g tryptophan; .8 g tyrosine; .8 g omega-3 fatty acids; 1.4 g omega-6 fatty acids. Calories from fat: 27 percent.

 ## Garlic Pork Roast

Using your slow cooker, this recipe is easy to throw together in the morning, and it makes a nice warm meal at the end of the day. Pork is listed as a possible headache trigger for some people on some food lists, so this would be an entrée option only for those who don't have a problem with pork.

Makes 6 servings

- 2 tsp. canola oil
- 1 2-lb. boneless pork loin roast, trimmed of any visible fat
- Salt and pepper (or lemon pepper)
- 4 sweet potatoes, cut into 2-inch pieces (about 4 cups altogether)
- 1 large onion, cut into 12 wedges
- 18 garlic cloves
- 1 2/3 cup homemade chicken or vegetable broth

1. Heat canola oil in a large nonstick skillet or frying pan. Season the roast all over with freshly ground salt and pepper, add to the pan, and brown on all sides.

2. Meanwhile, add the sweet potato, onion, and garlic to your slow cooker. Add the browned roast, and pour the broth evenly over the top. Cover slow cooker and cook on low for six to eight hours.
3. Let roast rest about 10 minutes before slicing. Serve sliced pork with a generous spoon of the vegetables. Drizzle with the pan juices.

Per serving: 331 calories; 35 g protein; 28 g carbohydrate; 8 g fat (2.3 g saturated fat, 3.8 g monounsaturated fat, 1.2 g polyunsaturated fat); 96 mg cholesterol; 4.3 g fiber; 247 mg sodium; 64 mg magnesium; .4 g tryptophan; 1.2 g tyrosine; .2 g omega-3 fatty acids; 1 g omega-6 fatty acids. Calories from fat: 22 percent.

Desserts

The following are basically dessert recipes without chocolate—one potential headache trigger that often finds its way into our favorite desserts. For good measure, these recipes will also be aspartame-free, because this is also a potential headache trigger for some people. Hopefully you'll enjoy these desserts so much, you won't even notice there is no cocoa or chocolate in them!

 **Blondies**

Trust me, I love fudgy brownies just as much as the next gal, but these blonde brownies, sans cocoa or chocolate, are truly delicious in their own right. A little bit of white chocolate chips help do the trick (they don't contain cocoa).

Makes 12 servings (1 square per serving)
- 1/2 cup whole wheat flour
- 1/2 cup unbleached white flour

- 1/2 tsp. baking powder
- 1/8 tsp. baking soda
- 1/2 tsp. salt
- 1/3 cup no-trans margarine (no more than 8 g fat/tbs.)
- 1 cup packed brown sugar
- 1 large egg (omega-3 enriched, if available)
- 1 tbs. pure vanilla extract
- 1/2 cup white chocolate chips

1. Preheat oven to 350 °F. Coat a 9-inch nonstick round or square cake pan with canola cooking spray.

2. Add the whole wheat flour, white flour, baking powder, baking soda, and salt to a separate bowl. Whisk together well, and set aside.

3. Melt the margarine in a small nonstick saucepan over medium heat. Stir in the brown sugar. Cook, stirring constantly, for about a minute. Let cool for a few minutes.

4. Add brown sugar mixture to a large mixing bowl. Add in the egg and vanilla, and beat on medium-low speed until well blended. On low speed, beat in the flour mixture, a little at a time, until all ingredients are blended. Stir in the white chocolate chips, and pour into the prepared pan.

5. Bake for about 25 minutes, or until blondies are done to your liking. Let cool about 10 minutes, then cut into 12 squares and serve!

Per serving: 190 calories; 3 g protein; 30 g carbohydrate; 6 g fat (1.9 g saturated fat, 1.7 g monounsaturated fat, 2 g polyunsaturated fat); 20 mg cholesterol; 1 g fiber; 184 mg sodium; 7 mg magnesium; .01 g tryptophan; .04 g tyrosine; .3 g omega-3 fatty acids; .7 g omega-6 fatty acids. Calories from fat: 30 percent.

 ## Peachy Cake

The best part about this cake is that you can use fresh, frozen, or canned peaches! Also, because the cake isn't too sweet, a slightly warm slice pairs nicely with a small scoop of light vanilla ice cream.

Makes 8 servings

- 3/4 cup whole wheat flour
- 3/4 cup unbleached white flour
- 2 tsp. baking powder
- 1/2 tsp. baking soda
- 1/4 tsp. salt
- 1 tsp. ground cinnamon
- 1 cup fat-free or light sour cream
- 2 large eggs (omega-3 enriched, if available)
- 2 cups peaches, peeled and diced into 1/2-inch cubes

Streusel topping

- 1/3 cup unbleached white flour
- 1 tbs. granulated sugar
- 1/2 tsp. vanilla extract (or vanilla powder)
- 3/4 tsp. ground cinnamon
- 2 tbs. no-trans margarine, frozen (no more than 8 g fat/tbs.)

1. Preheat oven to 350 °F. Coat a 9-inch square or round cake pan with canola cooking spray.
2. Add whole wheat flour, white flour, baking powder, baking soda, salt, and cinnamon to an 8-cup measure. Stir to blend well, and set aside.

3. Add sour cream and eggs to a large mixing bowl. Beat on medium speed to combine well. On low speed, slowly add in the dry ingredients. Beat until blended. Fold in the peaches, and then pour batter into the prepared pan.

4. Add ingredients for the streusel topping to a small food processor and pulse briefly to blend (or mix the ingredients together with a pastry blender until a crumb consistency is made). Sprinkle the topping on the cake batter. Bake for 40 minutes or until tester inserted in the center comes out clean. Serve cake slightly warm with light vanilla ice cream if desired.

Per serving: 205 calories; 7.5 g protein; 36 g carbohydrate; 3 g fat (.9 g saturated fat, 1.1 g monounsaturated fat, .9 g polyunsaturated fat); 56 mg cholesterol; 3 g fiber; 339 mg sodium; 6 mg magnesium; .02 g tryptophan; .08 g tyrosine; .3 g omega-3 fatty acids; .6 g omega-6 fatty acids. Calories from fat: 13 percent.

Easy as Pie Cherry Cobbler

There is absolutely no excuse for not making this cobbler recipe! All you need is three ingredients and about three minutes. If you want to make this recipe a little fancier, sprinkle 1/2 cup of coconut flakes over the top before baking.

Makes 15 servings

- 21-oz. can of cherry pie filling (other pie fillings can be substituted)
- 18.5-oz. box of yellow cake mix
- 1 1/4 cups light-colored, non-citrus fruit juice (apple or white grape, for example)

1. Preheat oven to 375 °F. Coat a 9 × 13-inch baking dish with canola cooking spray.
2. Spread pie filling evenly over the bottom of the prepared pan. Cover the filling with the cake mix. Drizzle the fruit juice evenly over the top, using a fork to help spread the mix evenly.
3. Bake for about 45 minutes, or until cake is thoroughly cooked in the center of the pan.

Per serving: 206 calories; 2 g protein; 40 g carbohydrate; 4 g fat (.6 g saturated fat, 1.7 g monounsaturated fat, 1.5 g polyunsaturated fat); 1 mg cholesterol; .6 g fiber; 230 mg sodium; 7 mg magnesium; .02 g trytophan; .05 g tyrosine; .1 g omega-3 fatty acids; 1.4 g omega-6 fatty acids. Calories from fat: 19 percent.

 ## Angel Food Cake Deluxe

Makes 12 servings
- 1 cup cake flour
- 1 cup granulated sugar
- 1/2 cup aspartame-free sugar substitute (Splenda, for example)
- 12 egg whites
- 1 1/2 tsp. vanilla extract
- 1 1/2 tsp. cream of tartar
- 1/2 tsp. salt

1. Preheat oven to 375 °F. Double-check that your angel food cake pan is clean and dry (any trace amounts of oil could cause your whipped egg whites to deflate).
2. Stir the flour, 1/4 cup of the sugar, and sugar substitute together in a medium-size bowl, and set aside.

3. In a large mixing bowl, whip the egg whites together with the vanilla, cream of tartar, and salt until medium-stiff peaks appear. Gradually add the remaining sugar (3/4 cup), while continuing to whip the egg whites to stiff peaks. When you think the egg whites have reached their maximum volume, gradually fold in the flour mixture one-third at a time. Be careful not to overmix. Pour the batter in the prepared pan.

4. Bake for 40 to 45 minutes or until cake springs back when touched. Remove the pan from the oven and turn it upside down on the neck of a bottle to prevent decompression while cooling. When completely cool, run a knife around the edge of the pan and invert onto a serving plate.

Per serving: 122 calories; 5 g protein; 25 g carbohydrate; .1 g fat (0 g saturated fat, 0 g monounsaturated fat, .05 g polyunsaturated fat); 0 mg cholesterol; .2 g fiber; 152 mg sodium; 6 mg magnesium; .06 g tryptophan; .16 g tyrosine; 0 g omega-3 fatty acids; .04 g omega-6 fatty acids. Calories from fat: 0 percent.

Variations of Angel Food Cake Deluxe

Cherry Angel Food Cake

Add 3/4 tsp. vanilla extract and 1/4 tsp. almond extract instead of the vanilla. Stir 1/2 cup sliced maraschino cherries (well drained) into the prepared angel food cake batter. Proceed to pour into the pan and bake.

Holiday Angel Cake

Stir 1 cup fresh cranberries (or 1/2 cup dried cranberries) and 1 tbs. finely chopped orange zest into prepared angel food cake batter. Proceed to pour into the pan and bake.

Strawberry Swirl Angel Food Cake

Warm 1/2 cup low-sugar strawberry preserves in the microwave, just enough to soften. Stir preserves into the batter using a knife to make swirls. Proceed to pour into the pan and bake.

Toss-and-Go Snack Recipe

Avoiding hypoglycemia can be a bit challenging when we are busy working or on the road. Of course, one option we always have is to make snacks at home to take with us. I can just picture us now with granola bars baking in the oven while we are getting ready for work . . . NOT! What about taking a couple of minutes to pour a few ingredients into a resealable plastic bag, tossing them together, and hitting the road? This way we can choose the ingredients and products that don't trigger headaches. Here is a quick recipe to get you started!

 **Pretzel Potpourri**

There's a little of everything in this quick snack mixture, including irresistible pretzels, a taste of cheese, a boost of bran, and the savory surprise of roasted soybeans.

Makes 7 servings (1/2 cup each)

- 1 cup firmly packed pretzel sticks
- 1 cup mini stoned wheat crackers (or reduced-fat cheese crackers if cheddar is not a trigger for you)
- 1 cup Multi-Bran Chex (or similar cereal)
- 1/2 cup roasted soybeans (unsalted or salted)

1. Toss: Add all of the ingredients into a resealable plastic bag, seal it well, and toss the ingredients together to blend.
2. Go: Take it with you on the road for a healthful, flavorful, high-fiber snack!

Per serving: 120 calories; 7 g protein; 18 g carbohydrate; 2.2 g fat (.5 g saturated fat, .4 g monounsaturated fat, .6 g polyunsaturated fat); 0 mg cholesterol; 3.5 g fiber; 225 mg sodium; 12 mg magnesium; 0 g tryptophan; 0 g tyrosine; .1 g omega-3 fatty acids; .3 g omega-6 fatty acids. Calories from fat: 17 percent.

Chapter 6

Supermarket Shopping Made Simple

The key to a chapter on smart supermarket shopping is to focus on how to avoid the ingredients and additives that may be headache triggers for you. So in this chapter you'll find lists of food products that contain MSG, nitrates/nitrites, and aspartame. I hope these lists will help you (we spent hours reading labels so hopefully you won't have to).

The other side to smart shopping is how to avoid buying and cooking high-fat foods, which may also encourage headaches in some people. Following, you will find some quick "low fat" shopping and cooking tips.

OK? On your mark, get set . . . shop!

Snack Attack Plan

Snacking has gotten a bad rap in the past, but it isn't the act of snacking that gets us in trouble. It's the types of food we tend to snack on that quickly put us into fat and calorie overload.

Our 2 Biggest Snack Mistakes

We tend to make two mistakes when we snack:

1. We choose calorie-dense high-fat or high-sugar snacks that, while containing a lot of calories for a relatively small amount of food, aren't satisfying in the long run. Such snacks include candy bars and chips. Aren't we still hungry after we eat a small bag of chips or a 2-oz. candy bar? Was that 320 calories well spent?

2. We choose high-carbohydrate snack foods, such as pretzels, bagels, or apples, which go through the digestive tract fairly quickly, staving off hunger for only a short amount of time. If we balance our quick carbs with some protein and fat, the snack will be more filling and satisfying, and will take longer to get through the digestive tract.

We can start by making smarter snack choices as much as possible. Here's how to do it:

*   Choose snacks that are higher in fiber and important nutrients.
*   Choose snacks that include carbohydrates with lower glycemic indexes, such as fruits, vegetables, whole grains, beans, and nuts, as tolerated.
*   Balance your snacks by including some lean protein and some of the more healthy-heart fats, such as monounsaturated fats and omega-3 fatty acids, to go with your carbs.

For example, adding plant foods that contribute some fat and/or protein into your snack recipes, such as nuts, soy, olive and canola oil, and avocado, for example, can help balance out the carbohydrate-rich ingredients.

F.Y.I. Soluble Fiber to the Rescue!

Foods rich in soluble fiber make for great snacks because soluble fiber leaves the stomach slowly, encouraging the production of better blood sugars and making you feel satisfied longer. Here are some possible snack ingredients that are high in soluble fiber:

- Peas and beans.
- Oats and oat bran.
- Barley.
- Some fruits, including apples, peaches, citrus fruits, mangos, plums, kiwis, pears, and berries.
- Some vegetables, including artichokes, celery root, sweet potatoes, parsnips, turnips, acorn squash, Brussels sprouts, cabbage, green peas, broccoli, carrots, cauliflower, asparagus, and beets.

Portable Snacks You Can Pack Anytime, Anywhere

1. Whole Grain Snacks

The following whole grain snacks travel well. They don't need refrigeration and don't get smashed easily (what more could you ask for?):

- Instant oatmeal (there are low-sugar types available).
- Snack bars high in fiber and low in sugar.
- Whole grain bagels.

- Whole grain cereals.
- Whole grain crackers (preferably with no trans fats and low in total fat).

2. Go Nuts! (If They Aren't One of Your Triggers)

An ounce of nuts is a satisfying snack, and you can take them anywhere! A serving of that size is about 170 calories, with 7 grams carbohydrates, 6 grams protein, 2 to 3 grams fiber (depending on the nut), and around 15 grams fat. (Generally, nuts contribute the better fats: monounsaturated fats and plant omega-3 and omega-6 fatty acids.)

3. Portable Fruit

Some pieces of fruit can travel well in your car or briefcase. They will come in handy for a quick pick-me-up, many offering just enough carbohydrates and a nice dose of fiber.

The following fruits travel well:

- Apples.
- Bananas.
- Dried fruits (as tolerated).
- Grapes.
- Kiwis.
- Oranges.
- Plums.

4. Eat Your Vegetables . . . As a Snack

Cut up fresh, raw vegetables and take them with you. Try snacking on:

- Baby carrots.
- Celery sticks.
- Jicama sticks.
- Sugar snap peas.

5. Try Trail Mix

The dried fruits in trail mix give you some fiber and carbohydrate calories, but the nuts help round the snack off with protein, fat, and more fiber. (This is a great option if dried fruits and nuts are not headache triggers for you.)

It's Not Easy Avoiding MSG!

If you think MSG could be a headache trigger for you, sit down and brace yourself, because you will not believe how many supermarket products contain this flavor-enhancer/additive! I've never seen any book or agency produce a copious list of products containing MSG, and now I know why. It was a huge task to do this. But we did it for you. We may have missed some products that contain MSG, and companies are constantly reformulating their products, so unfortunately you will still need to keep an eye out for MSG on all package labels.

Products Containing MSG

Note: The following is a list of products that list MSG as an ingredient on their labels at the time this book was written. There are products containing MSG that are not on this list. Always make sure to check labels of all food products for MSG before eating.

Included in this list is the sodium content in milligrams per serving size listed on the label of each product. Because MSG contributes sodium (monosodium glutamate), the sodium content may give us a good indication of how much MSG is added to a product.

Asian Food

LaChoy

Beef Chow Mein (800 mg/cup)
Chicken Chow Mein (1,240 mg/cup)

Chips

Bugles

Chili Cheese (310 mg/1 1/3 cup)
Salsa (320 mg/1 1/3 cup)
Southwest Ranch (310 mg/1 1/3 cup)

Cheetos

Asteroid Brand, Flamin' Hot (340 mg/cup)
Asteroids Brand, Cheese (320 mg/3/4 cup)
Original, Flamin' Hot (250 mg/21 pieces)

Chex Mix

Bold Party Blend (390 mg/1/2 cup)
Cheddar Cheese (370 mg/2/3 cup)
Hot'n Spicy (420 mg/2/3 cup)

Doritos*

Baked, Cooler Ranch (200 mg/15 chips)
Baked, Nacho Cheesier (220 mg/15 chips)
Go Snacks, Cooler Ranch (170 mg/46 chips)
Go Snacks, Nacho Cheesier (200 mg/46 chips)
Original, Black Pepper Jack (240 mg/12 chips)
Original, Cooler Ranch (170 mg/12 chips)
Original, Guacamole (230 mg/12 chips)
Original, Nacho Cheesier (200 mg/11 chips)
Original, Salsa (170 mg/12 chips)
Original, Salsa Verde (210 mg/12 chips)
Original, Spicier Nacho (210 mg/12 chips)
Rolitos, Cooler Ranch (250 mg/17 chips)
Rolitos, Nacho Cheesier (200 mg/17 chips)
Rolitos, Zesty Taco (140 mg/17 chips)
*Note:
The only Doritos that do not contain MSG is Toasted Corn.

Fritos

Flavor Twists, Honey BBQ (210 mg/23 chips)
Original, Chili Cheese (260 mg/31 chips)

Funyuns Onion-Flavored Rings (270 mg/13 rings)

Gardetto's Snack-ens

Original Recipe (330 mg/1/2 cup)
Original Recipe, Reduced Fat (320 mg/1/2 cup)

Lay's

Original, Cool Guacamole (250 mg/15 chips)
Original, Jalapeno (170 mg/15 chips)
Original, K.C. Masterpiece B.B.Q. (200 mg/15 chips)
Original, Kettle Cooked Mequite BBQ (210 mg/18 chips)
Stax, BBQ (190 mg/12 chips)
Stax, Cheddar (190 mg/12 chips)
Stax, Sour Cream and Onion (190 mg/12 chips)
Wavy, Hidden Valley Ranch (200 mg/12 chips)

Munchies

Flamin' Hot (190 mg/3/4 cup)
Go Snacks (230 mg/cup)
Kids Mix (240 mg/cup)

Planters Cheez Mania Cheez Balls (350 mg/34 balls)

Pringles

Cheezums (180 mg/14 chips)
Fiery Hot (200 mg/14 chips)
Original (160 mg/13 chips)
Ranch-Rageous (130 mg/14 chips)
Sour Cream and Onion (135 mg/14 chips)
Spicy Cajun (230 mg/14 chips)
Sweet Mesquite BBQ (200 mg/14 chips)

Ruffles

Original, Cheddar and Sour Cream (230 mg/11 chips)
Original, K.C. Masterpiece B.B.Q. (220 mg/15 chips)
Original, Sour Cream and Onion (190 mg/11 chips)
WOW, Cheddar and Sour Cream (230 mg/15 chips)

Tim's Cascade Style Chips

> Hot Jalapeno (130 mg/13 chips)
> Wasabi (220 mg/13 chips)

Tostitos

> Hint of Jalapeno (180 mg/6 chips)
> Hint of Lime (160 mg/6 chips)

Crackers

Keebler

> Cheez-Its, BBQ Cheddar (300 mg/25 pieces)
> Cheez-Its, Cheddar Jack (260 mg/26 pieces)
> Cheez-Its, Cheesy Sour Cream and Onion (250 mg/25 pieces)
> Cheez-Its, Parmesan and Garlic (240 mg/26 pieces)
> Cheez-Its, Party Mix (340 mg/1/2 cup)
> Cheez-Its, White Cheddar (280 mg/26 pieces)
> Munch'ems, Original (270 mg/39 pieces)

Kraft Cheese Nips

> Four Cheese (300 mg/26 pieces)
> Original (330 mg/12 pieces)

Nabisco Mixers

> Cheddar (350 mg/1/2 cup)

Orville Redenbacher Popcorn Mini Cakes

> Low-Fat Sour Cream and Onion (105 mg/8 cakes)

Quaker Quakes

> Cheddar Cheese (270 mg/25 pieces)
> Nacho Cheese (330 mg/25 pieces)
> Ranch (210 mg/10 cakes)
> Sour Cream and Onion (200 mg/10 cakes)

Ritz

> Cheddar (320 mg/14 chips)
> Sour Cream and Onion (330 mg/14 chips)

Triscuit

Cheddar (220 mg/6 pieces)

Dinner Mixes, Boxed

Betty Crocker*

Chicken Helper, Chicken and Potatoes Au Gratin (720 mg/serving)

Chicken Helper, Chicken Enchilada (690 mg/serving)

Chicken Helper, Chicken Teriyaki (810 mg/serving)

Hamburger Helper, Beef and Garlic Potatoes (860 mg/cup)

Hamburger Helper, Beef Pasta (740 mg/cup)

Hamburger Helper, Carb Monitor Cheeseburger Macaroni (800 mg/cup)

Hamburger Helper, Cheeseburger Macaroni (830 mg/cup)

Hamburger Helper, Cheesy Baked Potato (890 mg/cup)

Hamburger Helper, Cheesy Enchilada (680 mg/cup)

Hamburger Helper, Cheesy Nacho (740 mg/cup)

Hamburger Helper, Lasagna (850 mg/cup)

Hamburger Helper, Salisbury (730 mg/cup)

Hamburger Helper, Stroganoff (770 mg/cup)

Hamburger Helper, Three Cheese (900 mg/cup)

Pork Helper, Pork Chops and Stuffing (540 mg/cup)

Pork Helper, Pork Fried Rice (590 mg/cup)

Potato Mix, Butter and Herb (400 mg/1/2 cup, prepared)

Potato Mix, Deluxe Potatoes Creamy Scallops (270 mg/2/3 cup, prepared)

Potato Mix, Roasted Garlic (340 mg/1/2 cup, prepared)

Potato Mix, Scalloped (590 mg/1/2 cup, prepared)

Potato Mix, Sour Cream and Chives (330 mg/1/2 cup, prepared)

Tuna Helper, Cheesy Pasta (720 mg/cup, prepared)

Tuna Helper, Creamy Pasta (730 mg/cup, prepared)

Tuna Helper, Creamy Parmesan (780 mg/cup, prepared)

* Note: Betty Crocker offers many options that do not contain MSG, so give some of the flavors not listed here a look.

Campbell's Supper Bakes

> Cheesy Chicken With Pasta (950/1/6th box)
> Garlic Chicken With Pasta (870 mg/1/6th box)
> Lemon Chicken With Herb Rice (880 mg/1/6th box)
> Traditional Roast Chicken With Stuffing (880 mg/1/6th box)

Hungry Jack Side Dishes

> **Do not appear to contain MSG.**

Kraft Easy Mac*

> Extreme Cheese (620 mg/pouch)
> Tombstone Cheese Pizza (790 mg/pouch)
> ***Note:**
> **Of the varieties of Kraft Macaroni and Cheese, Easy Mac Original, Cooking Deluxe 2%, Cooking Deluxe Regular, Deluxe 4 Cheese, and Cooking Velveeta Shells and Cheese do not appear to contain MSG.**

Lipton Side Dishes*

> Smoked Chipotle Rice (770 mg/cup, prepared)
> ***Note:**
> **Most of the flavors in Lipton Side Dishes do not appear to contain MSG. The flavor listed was the exception.**

Mrs. Cubbison's

> **Do not appear to contain MSG.**

Pasta Roni*

> Angel Hair With Herbs (680 mg/cup)
> Angel Hair With Parmesan Cheese (750 mg/cup)
> Chicken (900 mg/cup)
> Chicken Broccoli Linguine (820 mg/cup)
> Fettucine Alfredo (920 mg/cup)
> Garlic Alfredo (1,010 mg/cup)
> Herb and Butter (710 mg/cup)
> ***Note:**
> **Garlic and Olive Oil, Shells and White Cheddar, and Homestyle Deluxe Four Cheese Past Roni do not appear to contain MSG.**

Rice-A-Roni

All of the flavors researched contain MSG.

Stove Top Stuffing*

Chicken (460 mg/1/2 cup, dry)
Chicken, Lower Sodium (250 mg/1/6th box)
Cornbread (490 mg/1/6th box)
Pork (450 mg/1/6th box)
San Francisco-Style (460 mg/1/6th box)
* Note:
Turkey Stove Top Stuffing does not appear to contain MSG.

Uncle Ben's Ready Rice

Does not appear to contain MSG.

Velveeta Boxed Potato Side Dishes

Does not appear to contain MSG.

Zatarain's

Brown Rice Jambalaya (450 mg/cup)
Chicken and Rice (790 mg/cup)
Dirty Rice (680 mg/cup, prepared)
Gumbo Mix With Rice (630 mg/cup)
Jambalaya (460 mg/cup, prepared)
Red Bean Seasoning (290 mg/1/2 cup)
Yellow Rice (920 mg/cup)
Yellow Rice, Ready to Serve (1,060 mg/cup, prepared)

Dips

Fritos

Chili Cheese (310 mg/2 tbs.)
Jalapeno and Cheddar Cheese (300 mg/2 tbs.)

Ruffles

French Onion Dip (230 mg/2 tbs.)
Ranch Dip (240 mg/2 tbs.)

Taco Bell

Salsa Con Queso (320 mg/2 tbs.)

Tostitos

Party Bowl Spicy Queso (250 mg/2 tbs.)
Party Bowl Zesty Beans and Cheese (260 mg/2 tbs.)
Salsa Con Queso (280 mg/2 tbs.)

Entrées, Canned

Campbell's

Chunky Chili: Does not appear to contain MSG.
SpaghettiOs: Does not appear to contain MSG.

Chef Boyardee

Mini Bites, Beef Ravioli and Meatballs
(890 mg/7.5-oz. container)
Original, Beef Ravioli in Tomato and Meat Sauce
(980 mg/7.5-oz. container)
Twistaroni, Cheesy Nacho (1,230 mg/cup)

Dennison's Chili

Does not appear to contain MSG.

Dinty Moore Microwavable Bowls

Chicken and Dumplings (1,010 mg/10 oz.)

Hormel Kids Kitchen

The 7.5-oz. containers do not appear to contain MSG.

Nalley Chili

Turkey With Beans (1,110 mg/cup)
Walla Walla Onion With Beans (1,060 mg/cup)
Original (1,140 mg/cup)

Stagg Chili

Does not appear to contain MSG.

Entrées, Frozen

Banquet

Chicken Fried Steak Meal (1,020 mg/meal)
Fried Chicken Meal (900 mg/meal)
Meatloaf Meal (980 mg/meal)
Mexican-Style Enchilada Combo Meal (1,750 mg/meal)
Swedish Meatballs (1,100 mg/meal)

Bird's Eye Voila Skillet Meals

Does not appear to contain MSG.

Boston Market

Entrées do not appear to contain MSG, but some do contain soy sauce.

Gorton's

Clams (330 mg/1/2 package)
Fish Fillets, Crispy Battered (780 mg/2 fillets)
Fish Fillets, Crunchy Golden (450 mg/2 fillets)
Fish Fillets, Garlic and Herb Crunchy Breaded (630 mg/2 fillets)
Fish Sticks, Crunchy Golden (380 mg/6 sticks)
Grilled Fillets, Garlic Butter (330 mg/fillet)
Grilled Fillets, Lemon Butter (380 mg/fillet)
Grilled Salmon, Classic Grilled (310 mg/fillet)
Popcorn Fish, Crispy (800 mg/11 pieces)
Shrimp Bowl, Alfredo (1,090 mg/bowl)
Shrimp Bowl, Fried Rice (1,700 mg/bowl)
Shrimp Bowl, Garlic Butter (1,030 mg/bowl)
Shrimp Bowl, Primavera (1,250 mg/bowl)
Tenders, Original Butter (770 mg/3.5 pieces)

Healthy Choice

Flavor Adventures, Mixed Grills, and Original do not appear to contain MSG, but some do contain soy sauce.

Hungry-Man

Angus Beef Meatloaf (1,740 mg/meal)
Beef Pot Roast (970 mg/meal)
Beer Battered Chicken and Cheese Fries (2,230 mg/meal)
Boneless White Meat Fried Chicken (1,900 mg/meal)
Buffalo-Style Chicken Strips (2,900 mg/meal)
Classic Fried Chicken (1,940 mg/meal)
Roasted Turkey Breast Meal (3,140 mg/meal)
Turkey Breast and Stuffing (1,080 mg/meal)

Lucca Ravioli

Does not appear to contain MSG.

Marie Callender's

Beef Stroganoff (1,550 mg/meal)
Country Fried Pork Chop (1,840 mg/meal)
Creamy Mushroom Chicken Pot Pie (820 mg/serving)
Salisbury Steak and Gravy (1,570 mg sodium/meal)
Southern Fried Chicken Tenderloins (1,465 mg/meal)
Sweet and Sour Chicken (850 mg/meal)

Michelina's

Does not appear to contain MSG.

Old El Paso

Burritos, Ground Beef, Rice, and Beans (400 mg/1/4 cup)
Burritos, Shredded Chicken (430 mg/1/4 cup)

Stouffer's

Family Style, Skillet Sensations, Lean Cuisine Skillet Sensations, and Lean Cuisine Original do not appear to contain MSG, but some do contain mushroom concentrate (a natural source of MSG) and/or soy sauce.

Swanson

Classic Fried Chicken (2,030 mg/meal)
Chicken Strips (940 mg/meal)
Angus Beef Salisbury Steak (750 mg/meal)

Uncle Ben's Rice Bowls

Do not appear to have MSG, but some do contain soy sauce.

Van de Kamp's

Fish Fillets, Crispy (260 mg/fillet)
Fish Fillets, Crunchy (350 mg/2 fillets)
Fish Sticks, Crisp and Healthy Breaded (420 mg/6 sticks)
Fish Sticks, Crunchy (370 mg/6 sticks)

Weight Watchers Smart Ones

Do not appear to have MSG, but some do have mushroom concentrate (a natural source of MSG) and/or soy sauce.

Lunch Meats

Oscar Meyer Lunchables

Cheesy Chip Nachos (1,220 mg/package)
Chicken Dunks (520 mg/package)

Mexican Food

La Victoria Enchilada Sauce, Green Chili, Mild (310 mg/1/4 cup)
Las Palmas Enchilada Sauce, Green Chili, Medium (260 mg/1/4 cup)

Salad Dressings and Bottled Sauces

Hellman's (or Best Foods)

Dippin' Sauce, Rockin' Ranch (130 mg/tbs.)

Hidden Valley

Buttermilk, Old-Fashioned (240 mg/2 tbs.)
Caesar With Crushed Garlic (270 mg/2 tbs.)
Ranch With Bacon (230 mg/2 tbs.)
Ranch With Garlic (270 mg/2 tbs.)
Ranch With Sundried Tomato and Feta (250 mg/2 tbs.)
Ranch, BBQ (220 mg/2 tbs.)

K.C. Masterpiece

> Dip & Top Sauce, Cool Ranch B.B.Q. (220 mg/ serving)
> Dip & Top Sauce, Honey Dijon (220 mg/serving)

Kraft

> CarbWell, Light Buttermilk Ranch (430 mg/2 tbs.)
> Light Done Right, Ranch (370 mg/2 tbs.)
> Ranch (310 mg/2 tbs.)
> Ranch Free (350 mg/2 tbs.)
> Ranch With Bacon (240 mg/2 tbs.)

Marzetti

> Ranch Dressing (210 mg/2 tbs.)
> Ranch, Fat Free (310 mg/2 tbs.)
> Ranch, Light (280 mg/2 tbs.)
> Ranch, Original (260 mg/2 tbs.)
> Ranch, Spicy (320 mg/2 tbs.)

Wishbone

> Just 2 Good, Ranch (290 mg/2 tbs.)
> Ranch, Original (200 mg/2 tbs.)
> Ranch-Up, Classic (230 mg/2 tbs.)
> Ranch-Up, Zesty (270 mg/2 tbs.)

Sausage

Hillshire Farm

> Cheddarwurst (700 mg/link)
> Lit'l Smokies (630 mg/6 links)
> Lite Polska Kielbasa (470 mg/2 oz.)
> Smoked Bratwurst (700 mg/link)
> Smoked Sausage, Turkey or Beef (540 mg/2 oz.)

Jimmy Dean

> All varieties have MSG.

Johnsonville

> Hot Links, Beef (630 mg/link)
> Smoked Bratwurst, Polish Sausage, Beef Bratwurst, Swisswurst, Beddar With Cheddar, and Smoked Sausage (640 mg/link)

Soups, Canned

Andersen's

Does not appear to contain MSG.

Campbell's

Carb Request, Chicken Broccoli Cheese (820 mg/cup)
Carb Request, Mediterranean-Style Meatball (890 mg/cup)
Carb Request, Savory Beef and Mushroom Medley (870 mg/cup)
Carb Request, Spicy Sausage With Chicken and Bell Pepper (840 mg/cup)
Chunky, Baked Potato With Cheddar and Bacon Bits (970 mg/cup)
Chunky, Beef Rib Roast With Potato and Herbs (890 mg/cup)
Chunky, Beef With White and Wild Rice (960 mg/cup)
Chunky, Chicken and Dumplings (890 mg/cup)
Chunky, Chicken Corn Chowder (900 mg/cup)
Chunky, Classic Chicken Noodle (860 mg/cup)
Chunky, Grilled Chicken With Vegetables and Pasta (850 mg/cup)
Chunky, Grilled Pork Loin With Vegetables and Beans (980 mg/cup)
Chunky, Hearty Bean and Ham (800 mg/cup)
Chunky, Salisbury Steak With Mushrooms and Onions (890 mg/cup)
Chunky, Savory Pot Roast (860 mg/cup)
Chunky, Sirloin Burger With Country Vegetables (850 mg/cup)
Chunky, Slow Roasted Beef With Mushrooms (830 mg/cup)
Chunky, Steak and Potato (920 mg/cup)
Chunky, Turkey Pot Pie (870 mg/cup)
Condensed, Alphabet Vegetable Made With Beef Broth (890 mg/1/2 cup, prepared)
Condensed, Alphabet Vegetarian Vegetable (790 mg/1/2 cup, prepared)
Condensed, Bean With Bacon (860 mg/1/2 cup, prepared)
Condensed, Beef Broth (860 mg/1/2 cup, prepared)

Campbell's (cont.)

Condensed, Beef Consomme (810 mg/1/2 cup, prepared)
Condensed, Chicken and Stars (940 mg/1/2 cup, prepared)
Condensed, Chicken Broth (770 mg/1/2 cup, prepared)
Condensed, Chicken With Rice (820 mg/1/2 cup, prepared)
Condensed, Cream of Asparagus (870 mg/1/2 cup, prepared)
Condensed, Cream of Celery (860 mg/1/2 cup, prepared)
Condensed, Cream of Chicken (870 mg/1/2 cup, prepared)
Condensed, Cream of Chicken, 98% Fat Free
(890 mg/1/2 cup, prepared)
Condensed, Cream of Mushroom
(870 mg/1/2 cup, prepared)
Condensed, Cream of Mushroom, 98% Fat Free
(900 mg/1/2 cup, prepared)
Condensed, Cream of Potato (880 mg/1/2 cup, prepared)
Condensed, Creamy Mushroom and Roasted Garlic
(790 mg/1/2 cup, prepared)
Condensed, Creamy Ranchero Tomato
(880 mg/1/2 cup, prepared)
Condensed, Double Noodle (830 mg/1/2 cup, prepared)
Condensed, Fun Shapes (780 mg/1/2 cup, prepared)
Condensed, Golden Mushroom (890 mg/1/2 cup, prepared)
Condensed, Kids Shapes (780 mg/1/2 cup, prepared)
Condensed, Minestrone (960 mg/1/2 cup, prepared)
Condensed, New England Clam Chowder
(880 mg/1/2 cup, prepared)
Condensed, Sports Pasta With Meatballs
(750 mg/1/2 cup, prepared)
Condensed, Vegetable Beef (890 mg/1/2 cup, prepared)
Healthy Request: Does not appear to contain MSG.
Kitchen Classics, Chicken Noodle (790 mg/cup)
Kitchen Classics, Lentil (750 mg/cup)
Kitchen Classics, New England Clam Chowder
(720 mg/cup)

Campbell's (cont.)

Select, Beef With Portabello Mushrooms and Rice (780 mg/cup)

Select, Chicken and Pasta With Roasted Garlic (840 mg/cup)

Select, Chicken Rice (920 mg/cup)

Select, Chicken With Egg Noodles (990 mg/cup)

Select, Herbed Chicken With Roasted Vegetable (890 mg/cup)

Select, Italian-Style Wedding (840 mg/cup)

Select, Mexican-Style Chicken Tortilla (890 mg/cup)

Select, Minestrone (790 mg/cup)

Select, New England Clam Chowder (870 mg/cup)

Soup at Hand, Chicken and Stars (960 mg/10.75-oz. container)

Soup at Hand, Chicken With Mini Noodles (980 mg/10.75-oz. container)

Soup at Hand, Creamy Chicken (970 mg/10.75-oz. container)

Soup at Hand, Creamy Mushroom (890 mg/10.75-oz. container)

Soup at Hand, Vegetable Beef (830 mg/10.75-oz. container)

Dominique's

Does not appear to contain MSG.

Progresso

Carb Monitor, Beef Vegetable (940 mg/cup)

Carb Monitor, Chicken Cheese Enchilada-Style (970 mg/cup)

Carb Monitor, Chicken Vegetable (860 mg/cup)

Carb Monitor, Tuscan-Style Meatball (860 mg/cup)

Traditional, Beef and Vegetable (850 mg/cup)

Traditional, Chickarina (1,010 mg/cup)

Traditional, Chicken and Homestyle Noodle (960 mg/cup)

Traditional, Chicken and Wild Rice (830 mg/cup)

Traditional, Chicken Barley (890 mg/cup)

Progresso (cont.)

Traditional, Chicken Pot Pie (970 mg/cup)
Traditional, Chicken Rice (820 mg/cup)
Traditional, Chicken Vegetable (830 mg/cup)
Traditional, Creamy Chicken Wild Rice (940 mg/cup)
Traditional, Hearty Chicken Rotini (940 mg/cup)
Traditional, Italian-Style Wedding (960 mg/cup)
Traditional, Lentil (880 mg/cup)
Traditional, New England Clam Chowder (790 mg/cup)
Traditional, Roasted Chicken Garden Herb (920 mg/cup)
Traditional, Roasted Garlic Chicken (970 mg/cup)
Traditional, Sirloin Steak and Vegetable (990 mg/cup)
Traditional, Slow-Cooked Vegetable Beef (990 mg/cup)
Traditional, Steak and Sautéed Mushroom (950 mg/cup)
Traditional, Steak and Homestyle Noodles (840 mg/cup)
Traditional, Turkey Noodle (1,060 mg/cup)
Traditional, Vegetarian Vegetable (990 mg/cup)

Snow's*

New England Clam Chowder, condensed (760 mg/1/2 cup, prepared)
*Note:
Ready-to-Serve New England Clam Chowder does not contain MSG.

Swanson*

Beef Broth, 99% Fat Free (890 mg/cup)
Beef Broth, Lower Sodium (440 mg/cup)
Chicken Broth, 99% Fat Free (980 mg/cup)
Vegetarian Vegetable Broth, 100% Fat Free (940 mg/cup)
*Note:
Natural Goodness Chicken Broth, 100% Fat-Free Chicken Broth, Certified Organic Chicken Broth, and Certified Organic Vegetable Broth do not appear to contain MSG.

Wolfgang Puck's Gourmet Soups

Do not appear to contain MSG.

Soup Mixes

Bear Creek

Hot and Sour (1,000 mg/cup, prepared)

Knorr

Recipe Classics, Cream of Broccoli
(730 mg/2 tbs.)
Recipe Classics, Cream of Spinach
(760 mg/2 tbs.)
Recipe Classics, Leek (810 mg/2 tbs.)
Recipe Classics, Vegetable (730 mg/2 tbs.)
Savory Soup, Beef (1,400 mg/1/2 cube)
Savory Soup, Chicken Noodle (650 mg/3 tbs.)
Savory Soup, Creamy Chicken With Rice
(860 mg/3 tbs.)
Savory Soup, Fish (980 mg/1/2 cube)
Savory Soup, French Onion (790 mg/2 tbs.)
Savory Soup, Mediterranean-Style Minestrone
(810 mg/3 tbs.)
Savory Soup, Vegetable Bouillon (830 mg/1/2 cube)

Lipton

Carb Options, Chicken Noodle (710 mg/envelope)
Carb Options, Mushroom (390 mg/2 tsp.)
Carb Options, Onion (400 mg/2 tsp.)
Recipe Secrets, Beefy Onion (610 mg/tbs.)
Recipe Secrets, Golden Onion (700 mg/1 2/3 tbs.)
Recipe Secrets, Onion (610 mg/tbs.)
Recipe Secrets, Onion Mushroom (640 mg/1 2/3 tbs.)
Recipe Secrets, Ranch (750 mg/tbs.)
Recipe Secrets, Savory Herb With Garlic (580 mg/tbs.)
Soup Secrets, Noodle Soup With Real Chicken Broth
(720 mg/cup, prepared)

Nile Spice Soup Cups

Do not appear to contain MSG.

Nissin

Cup Noodles: All flavors appear to contain MSG.

Top Ramen: All flavors appear to contain MSG.

Spice Hunter Soup Cups

Do not appear to contain MSG.

Wyler's

Mrs. Grass, Homestyle Vegetable (860 mg/1/4 packet)
Soup Starter, Beef Vegetable (650 mg/cup)
Soup Starter, Chicken Noodle (910 mg/cup)

Spices, Sauces, and Gravies

Franco-American

Beef Gravy, Ready to Eat (320 mg/1/4 cup)

Heinz

Homestyle Classic Chicken Gravy, Ready to Eat
(340 mg/1/4 cup)
Roasted Turkey Gravy, Ready to Eat
(270 mg/1/4 cup)
Savory Beef Gravy, Ready to Eat (210 mg/1/4 cup)

Knorr

Pesto Sauce, Dry (490 mg/2 tsp.)
Sundried Tomato Pesto, Dry (630 mg/tbs.)

McCormick

Bag'n Season, Pork Chops, Dry (590 mg/2/3 tsp.)
Bag'n Season, Swiss Steak, Dry (430 mg/tsp)
Beef and Herb Gravy, Dry (290 mg/2 tsp.)
Beef Stroganoff, Dry (350 mg/2 tsp.)
Brown Gravy, Dry (310 mg/tbs.)
Chicken Gravy, Dry (330 mg/2 tsp.)
Chicken Teriyaki Sauce Blend, Dry
(520 mg/1 1/3 tbs.)
Country Gravy Original, Dry (300 mg/1 1/3 tbs.)
Homestyle Gravy, Dry (280 mg/tbs.)
Pork Gravy, Dry (370 mg/tbs.)
Seasoned Meat Tenderizer, Dry (300 mg/1/4 tsp.)
Swedish Meatballs
(790 mg/2 tsp. meatball seasoning
and 1 tsp. sauce mix)
Turkey Gravy, Dry (350 mg/2 tsp.)

Find Certain Types of Products and You'll Find Nitrates/Nitrites

While reading labels, hunting for the words "nitrates" or "nitrites" so you can put them on your "Foods to Avoid" list, you can't help but notice that certain whole food categories are almost completely wiped out. You'll find nitrates/nitrites in most, if not all, bacon, pepperoni, processed luncheon meats, hot dogs, salami, jerky, ham, and most non-breakfast sausages. That's because the purpose of adding nitrates/nitrites has everything to do with curing meat. They add that pink color and that notable cured-meat flavor.

While I have compiled the following foods that contain nitrates/nitrites, always make sure and check the labels of products you aren't sure about because:

1. You might be looking at a brand that is unavailable in my supermarket and therefore has not been included in this list.

2. The food manufacturer could have changed its product formula, and now the product may contain nitrates/nitrites, whereas before it did not.

Bacon

Brands that contain nitrates/nitrites include:

Armour
Bar-S
Farmer John
Jennie-O
Johnsonville
Louis Rich

Beef

One brand that contains nitrates/nitrites is:

Shenson: Corned Beef Brisket and
Corned Beef Round

Ham

Nitrates/nitrites appear to be in pretty much all
hams. Specific brands I found include:

Cooks
Farmer John
Foster Farms
Hormel
Jennie-O
John Morrell

Frozen Food

Most frozen food products that contain bacon,
ham, pepperoni, or sausage are suspect. Here are
some specific examples of products in the frozen
food section that contain nitrates/nitrites:

Atkins Quick Cuisine Pizza: Smokehouse, Supreme,
and Pepperoni
Aunt Jemima Great Starts: Scrambled Eggs and Bacon
Banquet: Pepperoni Pizza
Barber Foods: Stuffed Chicken Breasts Cordon Bleu
Jimmy Dean Omelets: Ham and Cheese, and
Western-Style
Lean Pockets and Hot Pockets: Ham, Sausage, Bacon,
and Pepperoni
Oscar Mayer: Corn Dogs
State Farm: Beef Corn Dogs

Jerky

Every single brand of jerky I saw contained
nitrates/nitrites.

Luncheon Meats

Luncheon meats that contain nitrates/nitrites include pastrami, bologna, ham, hot dogs, salami, pepperoni, and turkey pepperoni. Specific brands I found include:

Aidell's: Prepackaged sausages
Lunchables: Pizza Cracker Stackers, Ham and Cheddar, All Star Hotdogs, Bologna and American Cracker Stacker, and Pizza

Note:
Healthy Choice and Hillshire Farm Oven-Roasted Turkey do not appear to contain nitrates/nitrites.

Pork

One brand that contains nitrates/nitrites is:

Cooks: Hickory Smoked Pork Hocks, Hickory Smoked Ham Shank, Pork Neck Bones, Bone-In Pork Shoulder, Bone-In Butt Portion, and Shank Portion

Sausage

Brands that contain nitrates/nitrites include:

Bar-S: Polish Sausage and Hot Cajun-Style Smoked Sausage
Busch: Beef Summer Sausage
Hillshire Farms: Lite Smoked Sausage, Smoked Sausage, Beef Smoked Sausage, Polska Kielbasa, Lite Polska Kielbasa, Cheddarwurst, Turkey Smoked Sausage, Lit'l Beef Smokies, Lit'l Polskas, Lit'l Weiners, Lit'l Cheddar Smokies, and Beef Hot Links
Jennie-O: Turkey Kielbasa
Johnsonville: Summer Sausage (Garlic, Beef, and Original), Smoked Brats, and Beef Brats

Note:
I didn't find any nitrates/nitrites in any "breakfast" sausages!

Seafood

One brand that contains nitrates/nitrites is:

Lascco: Sliced Smoked Nova Salmon

Soups

Most soups that contain bacon, ham, or sausage are suspect. The following soups contain nitrates/nitrites:

Campbells's: Split Pea With Ham and Bacon, Bean With Bacon, Grilled Chicken and Sausage Gumbo, and Hearty Bean and Ham
Note:
There appear to be no nitrates/nitrites in Andersen's Split Pea With Bacon Soup.

What You Need to Know About Aspartame When Shopping

Aspartame (a.k.a. NutraSweet and Equal) is one of the most popular artificial sweeteners around. It is made up of two amino acids (phenylalanine and aspartic) combined with methanol. It's mentioned in this chapter because it has been suspected of bringing on headaches in some people.

Seventy percent of America's aspartame intake comes directly from soft drinks. For the general population, the FDA set the acceptable daily intake (ADI) for aspartame at 50 milligrams per kilogram of body weight. This translates to 4 12-oz. cans of diet soda or 9 8-oz. glasses of fruit drink made from a powder per day. The ADI is the estimated amount of a substance per kilogram of body weight that a person can safely consume every day over a lifetime without risk.

There are two types of side effects from aspartame that have been noted for a small portion of the population:

1. Some people have claimed that they have had allergic reactions to aspartame (water accumulation in the lips, tongue, and throat; skin reactions; and respiratory problems), although this type of reaction has been difficult to confirm or reproduce in studies.

2. Some consumers have reported central nervous system side effects from aspartame consumption (headache, dizziness, and mood changes), but the Centers for Disease Control and Prevention (CDC) concluded in 1986, after reviewing 600 of these complaints, that there was no association. Yet, the Environmental Nutrition Newsletter reported in 1998 that the CDC was leaving open the possibility that a small group of people could be especially sensitive to aspartame.

If you think aspartame could be one of your headache triggers, these are the food products in my supermarket that contained it. But please note that there could be other aspartame-containing products not on this list, so be sure to check the labels of any products you aren't sure about.

Coffee

General Foods International: Sugar-Free Powdered Coffee and Chai Latte

Cookies

Murray: Sugar-Free Cookies

Frozen Desserts

Breyers: No Sugar Added Vanilla Ice Cream
Dole Fruit: Juice Frozen Bars, No Sugar Added
Healthy Choice: Premium Fudge Bars
Klondike: Slim-a-Bear Ice Cream Sandwiches
Popsicle Brand: Sugar-Free Popsicles

Fruit Beverages

Crystal Light: Powdered Mix
Ocean Spray: Diet Juices and Teas
Snapple: Diet Drinks
Tropicana Light: Premade Drinks (non-refrigerated)

Gelatin and Pudding

Jell-O: Gelatine, Sugar Free. Pudding, Sugar Free and Fat Free

Hot Cocoa

Albertson's Hot Cocoa Mix: No Sugar Added

Jams and Syrup

Cary's Sugar-Free Syrup
Smucker's: Sugar-Free Jellies
Spring Tree Syrup: Sugar Free and Low Calorie

Soda

7Up, Diet
A&W Root Beer, Diet
Barq's Root Beer, Diet
Coke, Diet
Dr. Pepper, Diet
IBC Root Bear, Diet
Mountain Dew, Diet
Orange Slice, Diet
Pepsi, Diet
Red Bull, Sugar Free
Sierra Mist, Diet
Sprite, Diet
Sunkist, Diet

Tea

Lipton: Diet Tea Powder

Yogurt

Dannon: Light'n Fit (6 oz.)
Yoplait Light: Fat Free

What Are Your Artificial Sweetener Options?

Most of us, in an effort to satisfy our sweet tooth and keep extra pounds off, want to have our cake and eat it, too. We want the sweetness of sugar without the calories. But if you are avoiding aspartame because you think it may be helping to trigger your headaches, the following are other artificial sweetener options you can choose from.

Acesulfame K (Sunette or Sweet One)

Acesulfame K ("K" refering to potassium) is 200 times sweeter than sugar, and was approved by the FDA as a table-top sweetener and additive for desserts, confections, and alcoholic beverages.

Pros

- Doesn't increase the risk of cancer (non-carcinogenic) according to government agencies.
- Doesn't produce a glycemic response when eaten.
- It can withstand high temperatures involved in cooking and baking.
- It isn't broken down by the body during digestion, and it is excreted from the body completely unchanged.
- It can increase the overall sweetness and decrease the bitter taste when paired with other artificial sweeteners.
- Use of acesulfame K within FDA guidelines appears to be safe for pregnant women.

Cons
- On its own, this artificial sweetener can have a bitter taste.
- The Washington-based consumer group Center for Science in the Public Interest believes the safety tests on acesulfame K were poorly conducted and were unable to properly assess the sweetener's cancer-causing potential.

Saccharin (Sweet'N Low)

Three hundred times as sweet as sugar, saccharin is an organic molecule produced from petroleum.

Pros
- Its sweetness is stable with heat.

Cons
- Due to bladder cancer found in male lab rats that were fed saccharin in huge amounts, the FDA proposed a ban on saccharin in 1977.
- Since 1981, saccharin has been listed as an "anticipated human carcinogen" in government reports. Although studies of high saccharin users (such as persons with diabetes) do not support an association between saccharin and cancer, subgroups such as male heavy smokers may be at increased risk.
- The American Medical Association's Council on Scientific Affairs suggested that parents and caregivers might want to limit young children's intake of saccharin because there is a limited amount of data available in this particular group.
- Saccharin can cross the placenta and linger in fetal tissue. The American Medical Association's Council on Scientific Affairs has suggested that women consider careful use of saccharin during pregnancy.

Sorbitol and Mannitol

These sugar alcohols, although found in nature (plant foods such as fruits and berries), are commercially made for use as alternative sweeteners. They are absorbed slowly, yet some of it isn't absorbed at all, which is why consuming large amounts can lead to diarrhea.

Pros
- Sorbitol has received the "Generally Recognized as Safe" designation from the FDA.

Cons
- Some people may experience a laxative effect from an amount of sorbitol greater than 49 grams and an amount of mannitol greater than 19 grams.

Sucralose (Splenda)

Splenda contains the artificial sweetener sucralose, as well as maltodextrin, which adds bulk to the mixture (and possibly 12 calories per tablespoon) so it can be measured cup-for-cup for sugar in recipes. Sucralose is 600 times sweeter than sugar. To make sucralose, they take a cane sugar molecule and substitute three hydrogen–oxygen groups with three chlorine atoms.

Baking tip: I have been experimenting with Splenda in recipes lately and I have found the results usually successful when I use half real sugar and half Splenda as the sweetner in a recipe.

Pros
- Sucralose has no calories, is not considered a carbohydrate by the body, and doesn't have any effect on blood sugar levels.
- You can bake with Splenda. Heat doesn't take away from the sweet taste.

- When it comes to baking and cooking, Splenda appears to be the best artificial sweetener for the job.
- Of all the artificial sweeteners, Splenda has caused the least controversy from watchdog or consumer groups.
- After more than 110 studies (including animal and human studies), the FDA concluded that sucralose was shown to have no toxic or carcinogenic effects, does not alter DNA, and does not pose reproductive or neurological risk to humans.
- A recent British study on a range of sucralose intake in humans concluded there is no indication that negative effects on human health would occur from frequent or long-term exposure to sucralose at the higher levels of intake.[1]

Cons
- The bulking agents used in artificial sweetener products such as Splenda can contribute around 12 calories per tablespoon. (The package does not list these calories).
- Splenda can change the texture in baking recipes and can add an "artificial" taste to the food when used 100 percent as the sweetener in the recipe.
- Some critics claim that preliminary animal research has shown organ damage.

Stevioside

Stevioside is an herb that is 250 to 300 times sweeter than sugar and is calorie-free. It comes from the stevia plant in South America, and you can find it in the herbal section of health food stores sold as a powdered extract or in liquid form.

Pros

- Stevioside has been used in South America for centuries. It's been used in Japan for the past 30 years as well.

Cons

- Stevioside has not gone through the FDA approval process for use as a sweetener.

- Stevioside is sold as a dietary supplement in the United States, not as an official artificial sweetener. Supplements are not well regulated by the government and there is the possibility that they are not pure.

- Research in the 1980s suggested that when stevioside was tested with a certain bacteria, it could alter DNA. The FDA believes the safety of stevioside has not been proven yet.

Chapter 7

Restaurant Do's and Don'ts

R estaurant and fast-food dining has a few major pitfalls: The food is most often high in fat, and the portions are often huge. Some restaurants may also be using an additive that you have a sensitivity to (MSG, nitrites/nitrates, and aspartame, for example).

Following the 10 Food Steps to Freedom is challenging enough in the safety and comfort of your own home, but what about when you are out and about? We go to restaurants and fast-food chains (more often than we admit). We go on road trips, business trips, and vacations. No matter where we go or where we choose to catch a bite, our headache food triggers and food sensitivities go with us, too.

It goes without saying that you should only consider MSG-free restaurants. Also, avoid restaurants that cannot cater to your special requests for food preparations because they serve already-prepared foods (buffet-style restaurants or diners, for example).

You already know basically which foods or ingredients to avoid if you have a sensitivity to caffeine, tyramine, nitrates/nitrites, MSG, and aspartame. You already know which magnesium-rich foods to choose if hormonal headaches are your focus. But I can offer you a bit of help when it comes to eating out by stressing the "avoid higher-fat meals" and "avoid skipping meals" commandments.

Here are the restaurant do's and don'ts to help you avoid high amounts of fat:

Restaurant Do's

- Plan ahead and do your homework on restaurants. Know which restaurants have healthier options on the menu, and find out by calling ahead if they can make substitutions or take special requests on food preparation.

- Select fresh fruits or vegetables when you are given the option with your meal, and ask that fat not be added to your vegetables before it gets to the table. A 2004 study from St. Louis University's School of Public Health found that the more often parents ate out, the lower their intake of fruits and vegetables were (excluding French fries). You can correct this by going out of your way to order fresh fruits and vegetables!

- Enjoy broth-based soups rather than creamy soups when given the option with your meal. There is a huge difference in calories and fat grams between minestrone and chicken noodle–type soups compared with cheesy potato or cream of broccoli. (A cup of minestrone contains around 130 calories and 3 grams fat. Compare that to a cream-based soup made with half-and-half, which contains around 315 calories and 27 grams fat per cup.)

- Order salad dressings on the side so you know exactly what amount you are eating (if it's a high-fat dressing, try to keep to 1 tablespoon). Ask if they have a reduced-fat dressing. If they do and it appeals to you, you can get away with adding 2 tablespoons to your salad. High-fat salad dressings usually contain around 8 grams fat per tablespoon, and reduced-fat dressings tend to contain around 4 grams fat per tablespoon.

- Go for the grilled foods, such as grilled chicken, grilled shrimp, and roasted turkey sandwiches, especially if the alternative is a fried chicken sandwich or battered and fried shrimp.

- Look for menu entrées that are described as broiled, barbecued, grilled, poached, steamed, or roasted. These descriptors tend to indicate healthier menu options.

- Enjoy a lean hamburger in the smallest size available when you are in the mood for a hamburger. Avoid the "double burgers" or 1/3- or 1/2-pound sizes.

- Take half of your meal home when you are served large restaurant portions.

- Opt for petite portions of meat or casserole dishes when given the choice on the menu.

- Choose the healthier side dishes, such as in-season vegetables and broth-based soups. (You are often given a choice on the menu.)

- Feel free to order an appetizer instead of an entrée. If there is an appetizer that really appeals to you, you can often enjoy the appetizer as your entrée, then supplement it with a nice broth-based soup, whole wheat bread, or a green salad with low-fat dressing.

- When you find yourself "having" to try a particular restaurant dessert, share your dessert with your date or the entire table. That way you get to sample your irresistible dessert, yet not add too many grams of fat to your meal total.

- Order the baked potato instead of the French fries, but watch out: The toppings can add up quickly. Keep the bacon bits and cheese to a minimum, and don't even think about butter. Try a dollop of sour cream instead. One-eighth cup of sour cream will add 59 calories and 5.5 grams fat compared to 1 tablespoon of butter, which adds 102 calories and 12 grams fat.

- Order your egg dish or omelet with egg substitute (or egg whites, if desired) instead of regular eggs if at all possible. A 2-egg omelet made with whole eggs is 150 calories and 10 grams fat. Compare that to a 2-egg omelet made with egg substitute, which totals 60 calories and 0 grams fat.

- Order any sauces on the side that come with your entrée. That way if they are buttery, creamy, or oily, you can add them carefully. One tablespoon of any kind of sauce, no matter how buttery or rich, won't get you into too much trouble (up to 12 grams fat). One-quarter cup, however, can be down right dangerous (up to 48 grams fat).

- Look for entrées that come with tomato-based sauces, such as marinara or salsa. These tend to be low in fat and calories.

- Share an entrée with a friend. Waiters are usually happy to bring an extra plate, and many restaurants will even split the entrée before they bring it to your table.

Restaurant Don'ts

- Don't supersize anything. In fact, enjoy the small size of everything (if you have to have the fries, just order the small size). Don't tell McDonald's or Wendy's, but I often order the kid meals (I'm over 40). I find it's actually the perfect portion size for many people.

- Don't go crazy with higher-fat garnishes and toppings, such as mayo-based sauces, sour cream, guacamole, grated cheese, and bacon bits. Keep them a "garnish" by using no more than a tablespoon of each. A tablespoon of each will add around:

- Mayo: 98 calories and 11 grams fat.
- Sour cream: 30 calories and 3 grams fat.
- Guacamole: 17 calories and 1.7 grams fat.
- Grated cheese: 28 calories and 2.3 grams fat.
- Bacon bits: 20 calories and 1.5 grams fat.

- Read the menu carefully, and don't order items described as fried, crispy, creamy, au gratin, battered, or breaded. These descriptors tend to tell a story of higher-fat and higher-calorie menu choices.

- Don't order your hamburger or sandwich with the "special sauce" or mayonnaise. You can add lower-fat condiments such as ketchup or mustard at the table or at home.

- Don't order the battered and fried entrees at Chinese/ Asian restaurants. Instead, enjoy the stir-fried dishes that come with plenty of vegetables. You can also ask for your stir-fried dish to be prepared with "light" oil. If you do decide to enjoy one of the battered and fried Chinese/Asian entrées, make sure to enjoy it with a very low-fat side dish, such as steamed brown rice or steamed vegetables, to balance it out.

- Skip the deep-fried tortilla when ordering Mexican food at a restaurant or fast-food chain (for example, avoid crispy tacos, tostadas, or flautas). Order "soft" tacos or enchiladas. Also, make sure to ask them not to fry them before preparing your meal. A soft corn tortilla contains about 66 calories and .8 grams fat, while a crispy or fried corn tortilla can contain around 127 calories and 7.5 grams fat.

- Don't go to a restaurant or fast-food chain totally famished. You are more likely to order too much. You are also more likely to eat fast and in larger amounts. Eat a piece of fruit, some whole grain crackers, or trail mix before you go just to take the edge off your extreme hunger.

Road Trip Do's and Don'ts

The two biggest problems if you spend a lot of time on the road is trying not to skip meals and making healthy choices when you do get the chance to eat. So, to help you hit the road as headache-free as possible, here are the 4 Healthy Eating Commandments to Eating and Driving.

1. Portion Snacks So It Isn't a Feeding Free-For-All

One of the problems with eating and driving is the tendency to overeat. You are doing a few things at once and you may not be paying attention to the act of eating and the amount you are consuming. The answer? Package take-along snacks in snack-size resealable plastic bags to keep your portions moderate. Because driving is rather monotonous, eating while driving can be mindless as well. If you are snacking from a large bag or box of snack food, you could be at the bottom before you know it!

2. Rehydrate With Smart Beverages

Sometimes for me, just about the only time I get a chance to concentrate on sipping water and hydrating myself is while I'm driving! Use this driving opportunity wisely by drinking decaffeinated, no-, or low-sugar beverages. Watch the caffeine—it's an intestinal and bladder stimulator as well as a possible headache-trigger. Overdosing on caffeine will make you over-visit the restrooms along the way.

3. Eat Balanced Meals and Snacks That Curb Hunger

Meals and snacks that feature smart carbs (higher in fiber with mostly complex carbohydrates, not refined) and are balanced with some protein and fat will tend to be more satisfying in the stomach. They will scare off hunger longer than a meal or snack that is mostly refined carbohydrates. One example of a balanced meal would be a bean and cheese burrito or a turkey and avocado sandwich on whole grain bread.

4. B.Y.O.S. (Bring Your Own Snacks)

By planning ahead, we can stack the snack deck in health's favor. We can keep ourselves comfortable, refreshed, and well nourished while we drive without driving our healthy-eating intentions off a cliff. It is all too easy to grab a bag of chips or a box of crackers or cookies to eat in the car. Change the types of food you take with you, though, and you are not only adding more nutrients to your day, you are successfully avoiding a big collision of extra fat and calories.

What are good driving food selections? Fruits and vegetables would be at the top of my list. Lower-fat dairy products work well, too, along with whole grains and nuts. Sandwiches with lean meats, such as a turkey breast sandwich on whole grain bread, are also a nice addition if you can keep them well chilled in the car. (Think about investing in a car cooler or ice chest to keep your snacks cool!)

Take-Along Snacks

Take-along snacks must be easy to carry, easy to eat on the road, and reasonably healthy. What does this mean? It means they can't have too much fat or sugar. This rules out many of the snacks we are so tempted to take with us, such as crackers, cheese snacks, gummy fruit snacks, chewy granola bars, and fruit-filled breakfast bars—all of which list sugar as their first ingredient.

- **Crackers.** Try to find brands that use canola oil and contain some fiber.

  - Pretzel rods: First three ingredients are flour, water, and partially hydrogenated soybean oil. Three rods contain 120 calories; 1 g fat; 0 g saturated fat; 1 g fiber.

  - Triscuit, reduced fat: First three ingredients are whole wheat, partially hydrogenated soybean oil, and salt. Seven wafers contain 120 calories; 3 g fat; .5 g saturated fat; 4 g fiber.

- **Nature Valley Crunchy Granola Bars.** These are the only granola bars I found that use canola oil and don't list sugar as the first ingredient!

  - Oats 'N Honey or Cinnamon: First three ingredients are whole grain rolled oats, sugar, and canola oil. Two bars give you 180 calories; 6 g fat; .5 g saturated fat; 2 g fiber.

  - Peanut Butter: First three ingredients are whole grain rolled oats, sugar, and canola oil. Two bars give you 180 calories; 6 g fat; 1 g saturated fat; 2 g fiber.

- **Fresh Fruit.** I think the trick to making fresh fruit appealing on a road trip is to keep it cold—there's nothing worse than hot, mushy fruit. So if you freeze some grapes or keep your melon balls, apple wedges, or orange wedges well chilled in the car, taking them out for a nice afternoon snack will be particularly refreshing. Because fruits don't have a lot of fat, they don't contain large amounts of omega-6 nor omega 3 fatty acids. Cantaloupe, however, contains a nice little dose of omega-3s.

- Orange segments (chilled): 1 cup contains 85 calories; 0 g fat; 3.5 g fiber; 30% daily value of folic acid; 160% daily value of vitamin C; 9% daily value of calcium.
- Cantaloupe cubes (chilled): 1 cup contains 56 calories; .4 g fat; 1.3 g fiber; 64% daily value of vitamin A; 15% daily value of folic acid; 113% daily value for vitamin C.

- **Dried Fruit Snacks.**
  - Sun-Maid Fruit Bits: 1/4-cup gives you 120 calories; 0 g fat; 2 g fiber.
  - Del Monte Fruit & Nut Snacks, Cranberry Medley: 1 pack gives you 120 calories; 5 g fat; 1 g fiber.
  - Del Monte Fruit Snacks, Tropical Mix: 1 pack gives you 90 calories; 1 g fat; 1 g fiber.

- **Portable Veggies.**
  - Edamame: Go figure! These boiled soybeans in pods are all the rage—even celebrities have been seen munching on them. Bags are available in the frozen food section of some supermarkets.

Before you leave on your trip, microwave a 16-ounce bag of edamame in 1/4 cup water in a covered microwave-safe dish on high for about six to eight minutes. Drain and let them cool in the refrigerator overnight. Pour them in a resealable plastic bag and take them on the road for a nice, sustainable, nutritious snack (keep chilled, if possible). Popping the soybeans from the pod (discard the pods) and eating them keeps you busy on the road (but not if you're the driver). This keeps you from eating too much too fast, as is the case with cookies and chips. Soybeans do contain some omega-6 fatty acids, but they also contain some omega-3s.

A half cup of shelled beans (about 1 1/8 cup beans in pods) contains 90 calories; 2 g fat; 0 g saturated fat; 8 g fiber; 10 g protein.

- Baby carrots: Ice-cold baby carrots are a refreshing afternoon snack. They are crunchy, taste good, and are easy to eat out of the bag. You can find big or little bags of prewashed baby carrots in the produce section of most supermarkets. Keep them refrigerated if possible.

Ten baby carrots contains 38 calories; .5 gram fat; 3 grams fiber; 25% daily value of vitamin A; 18% daily value of folic acid; 14% daily value of vitamin C.

- **Snackable Breakfast Cereals.** Tasty cereals that are not too big on fiber include:
  - Cheerios, Apple Cinnamon: 3/4 cup gives you 120 calories; 1.5 g fat; 1 g fiber; 13g sugar.
  - Cinnamon Life: 3/4 cup gives you 120 calories; 1 g fat; 2 g fiber; 9 g sugar.

Serious higher-fiber cereals include:
- Kellogg's Raisin Bran: 1 cup gives you 190 calories; 1.5 g fat; 7 g fiber; 19 g sugar (this includes sugar from the raisins).
- Quaker Squares: 1 cup gives you 230 calories; 2.5 g fat; 5 g fiber; 14 g sugar.
- Chex, Multi Bran. 1 cup gives you 200 calories; 1.5 g fat; 8 g fiber; 12 g sugar.
- Kellogg's Frosted Mini Wheats: 24 biscuits give you 200 calories; 1 g fat; 6 g fiber; and 12 g sugar.

 Chapter Notes

Chapter 1

1. "Comorbidities are Common With Migraine." *Clinical Psychiatry News.* 32 (2004): 4.

2. MacGregor, E. *Neurology.* 63 (2004): 351–353.

3. Silberstein, S.D. *Neurology.* 63 (2004):261–269.

4. *European Journal of Neurology.* 11 (2004): 475–477.

5. Evers, S. et al. *Cephalalgia.* (2004).

Chapter 2

1. Mannix L.K., M. Diamond, and E. Loder. "Women and Headache: A Treatment Approach Based on Life Stages." *Cleveland Clinic Journal of Medicine.* 69 (2002): 488–500.

2. Environmental Nutrition. "New Study: What You Eat May Affect Hay Fever Symptoms." *Environmental Nutrition Newsletter.* (2004).

Chapter 3

1. Demeule M. et al. "Assessment of Dietary Triggers for Migraine Patients." *JADA*. 98 (1998).

2. Peatfield, R.C. "Relationships Between Food, Wine, and Beer-Precipitated Migrainous Headaches." *Headache*. 35 (1995): 355–357.

3. Bic, Z. et al. "The Influence of a Low-Fat Diet on Incidence and Severity of Migraine Headaches." *J. Women's Health*. 8 (1999): 623–630.

4. Leira, R. et al. "Diet and Migraine." *Rev. Neurol*. 24 (1996): 534–538.
   Jo Demeule, M. et al. "Assessment of Dietary Triggers for Migraine Patients." *Journal of the American Dietetic Association*. 98 (1998).

5. Blau, J.N. "What Some Patients Can Eat During Migraine Attacks: Therapeutic and Conceptual Implications." *Cephalalgia*. 4 (1993): 293–295.

6. MacReady, Norra. "Exercise Boosts Mood, Stamina in Alzheimer's Patients." *Internal Medicine News*. 37 (2004).

7. Stay, R. et al. "The Effect of a Carbohydrate-Rich Diet on Weight Loss Among Obese Females Who Overeat When Stressed." *Journal of the American Dietetic Association*. 95 (1995).

8. Sherman, C. "Omega-3 Effect on Mood Seems to Be Dose Dependent—In a Different Way." *Family Practice News*. 34 (2004).

9. Environmental Nutrition. "Experts Say Food, Mood Linked." *Environmental Nutrition Newsletter*. (2003).

Additional Sources:

Alcohol Clin. Exp. Res. 25 (2001): 487–495.

Braz, J. *Med Biol*. Res. 31 (1998): 1517–1527.

Can. J. Physiol. Pharmacol. 69 (1991): 893–903.

J. Affect. Disord. 69(2002): 15–29.

Lambert, Gavin. *Lancet*. December 2002 issue.

Mayo Clinic Women's Health Source, June 2002 issue.

Med. J. Aust. 173 (2000): 104–105.

Nutr. Neurosci. 5 (2002): 363–374.

Obes. Res. 4 (1995): 477–480.

Public Hlth. Nutr. 5 (2002): 427–431.

Chapter 4

1. Monell Chemical Senses Center in Philadelphia.

2. FDA's Center for Drugs and Biologics.

3. Griffiths, R. et al. *Psychopharmacology* (2004).

4. Chanmugam, P. et al. "Did Fat Intake in the United States Really Decline Between 1994 and 1996?" *Journal of the Dietetic Association.* 103 (2003).

5. Patterson, R.E. et al. "Changes in Food Sources of Dietary Fat in Response to an Intensive Low-Fat Dietary Intervention: Early Results From the Women's Health Initiative." *Journal of the Dietetic Association.* 103 (2003).

6. *Headache Quarterly* 7 (1996): 239–249.

7. *Clin. Exp. Allergy.* 23 (1993): 982–985.

8. *Pediatr. Med. Chir.* 15 (1993): 57–61.

9. *Panminerva Med.* 44 (2002): 27–31.

10. *Rev. Neurol.* 24 (1996): 534–538.

Additional Sources:

Reports from the Headache Resource Center of Providence Everett Medical Center in Washington state.

Millichap, J.G. et al. "The Diet Factor in Pediatric and Adolescent Migraine." *Pediatr. Neurol.* 28 (2003): 9–15.

National Headache Foundation document titled "Diet and Headache" (*www.headaches.org/consumer/topicsheets/ diet_headache.html*).

Chapter 6

1. Baird I.M., et al. "Repeated Dose Study of Sucralose Tolerance in Human Subjects." *Food Chem. Toxicol.* 38 (2000): 123–129.

Additional Sources:

American Dietetic Association. "Position of the American Dietetic Association: Use of Nutritive and Nonnutritive Sweeteners." *Journal of the American Dietetic Association.* 98 (1998).

Baird I.M. et al. "Repeated Dose Study of Sucralose Tolerance in Human Subjects." *Food Chem. Toxicol.* 38 (2000): 123–129.

Blackburn G.L. et al. "The Effect of Aspartame as Part of Multidisciplinary Weight-Control Program on Short- and Long-Term Control of Body Weight." *American Journal of Clinical Nutrition.* 65 (1997): 409–418.

Bradstock M. et al. "Evaluation of Reactions to Food Additives: The Aspartame Experience." *American Journal of Clinical Nutrition.* 43 (1986): 464–469.

Council on Scientific Affairs. "Aspartame: Review of Safety Issues." *Journal of the American Medical Association.* 254 (1985): 400–402.

Council on Scientific Affairs. "Saccharin: Review of Safety Issues." *Journal of the American Medical Association.* 254 (1985): 2,622–2,624.

Environmental Nutrition. "Sucralose: How Sweet It Is or Perhaps Isn't?" *Environmental Nutrition Newsletter.* (2002).

Environmental Nutrition. "Sugar Substitutes Still Have Sour Image, as Safety Issues Simmer." *Environmental Nutrition Newsletter.* (1998).

Glossary

aura migraine A migraine that produces symptoms including seeing bright lights, distorted vision, and wavy or jagged lines.

aromatherapy The practice of using the scents from plant oils to alleviate the symptoms of an illness.

aspartame An ingredient used in artificial sweeteners.

biofeedback The practice of using electrodes attached to the body to determine if a particular headache treatment is working.

carbohydrate Also known as a carb, this is a compound that is found in many foods and provides energy to the body.

cluster headaches An extremely painful type of headache that appears as a group, or cluster, of smaller headaches.

feverfew An herb that is believed to be good for treating headaches.

flaxseed A type of seed that provides many headache-curing nutrients.

hay fever An allergic reaction to pollen and other natural airborne particles.

hormone A chemical produced by the body's cells that can affect headaches.

hypnosis The practice of treating ailments by inducing the patient into a subconscious state.

hypoglycemia A severe lack of sugar in the blood.

MSG Short for monosodium glutamate, this chemical is believed to be a headache trigger for some.

omega-3 Fatty acids that are found in some fish.

For More Information

American Council for Headache Education (ACHE)
19 Mantua Road
Mount Royal, NJ 08061
(800) 255-ACHE (2243)
E-mail: achehq@talley.com
Web site: http://www.achenet.org
The ACHE is a nonprofit organization that works with
patients and doctors to help people participate in their
own care.

National Headache Foundation (NHF)
428 West Saint James Place, 2nd Floor
Chicago, IL 60614-2750
(800) 843-2256
Web site: http://www.headaches.org
The NHF is a nonprofit organization designed to educate
people about headaches by sending out lists of doctors,
publishing a quarterly newsletter, and organizing
support groups.

World Headache Alliance
612 Thornwood Avenue
Burlington, ON L7N 3B8
Canada
+ 1 905 257 6229
E-mail: mail@w-h-a.org
Web site: http://www.w-h-a.org
The World Headache Alliance is based in Canada and provides education and support to headache sufferers the world over.

Web Sites

Due to the changing nature of Internet links, Rosen Publishing has developed an online list of Web sites related to the subject of this book. This site is updated regularly. Please use this link to access the list:

http://www.rosenlinks.com/tmwe/hemi

For Further Reading

Johnson, Michael L. *What Do You Do When the Medications Don't Work? A Non-Drug Treatment of Dizziness, Migraine Headaches, Fibromyalgia, and Other Chronic Conditions*. Appleton, WI: Jokamar-Jenake Publishing, 2003.

Landau, Elaine. *Head and Brain Injuries*. Berkeley Heights, NJ: Enslow Publishers, Inc., 2002.

Marks, David R., and Laura Marks. *The Headache Prevention Cookbook: Eating Right to Prevent Migraines and Other Headaches*. Boston, MA: Houghton Mifflin, 2000.

Mauskop, Alexander, and Barry Fox. *What Your Doctor May Not Tell You About Migraines: The Breakthrough Program That Can Help End Your Pain*. New York, NY: Warner Books, 2000.

Roberts, Teri. *Living Well with Migraine Disease and Headaches : What Your Doctor Doesn't Tell You . . . That You Need to Know*. New York, NY: Collins, 2005.

Stafford, Diane, and Jennifer Shoquist. *Migraines for Dummies*. Hoboken, NJ: Wiley, 2003.

Young, William B., Stephen D. Silberstein, and Austin J. Sumner. *Migraine and Other Headaches*. New York, NY: Demos Medical Publishing, 2006.

Votava, Andrea. *Coping with Migraines and Other Headaches*. Rev. ed. New York, NY: Rosen Publishing Group, 2000.

ⓘ Index

A

"aura," migraine, 18–19
abortive medications, 19
acesulfame K, 177–178
additive-induced headaches,
  42–43
additives, avoiding certain,
  110–111
alcohol, reducing intake, 71
allergies and headaches,
  44–45
alternative therapies, 26–27
Angel Food Cake Deluxe,
  145–146
antinausea medications, 19
aromatherapy, 65
artificial sweetener options,
  177–181
aspartame, 104, 174
  as migraine trigger, 58
  products containing,
    175–176

B

beverages,
  dehydrating, 111
  to avoid dehydration, 188
biofeedback, 27–28
Blondies, 141–142
blood pressure, lowering to
  reduce headaches, 58
blood vessel reaction during
  headaches, 18
Botox, as treatment, 28–29
"brain freeze," 61
breakfast, balanced, 73
breathing exercises, 65
brunch recipes, 119–125

C

Cady, Roger, M.D., 8
caffeine and rebound
  headaches, 45–46
caffeine as migraine trigger,
  53, 55

About the Author

Elaine Magee, M.P.H., R.D., is the author of the celebrated syndicated column "The Recipe Doctor." Elaine is a regular contributor to *Parenting* and *Woman's Day* and is the author of eighteen books on nutrition and cooking, including *The Recipe Doctor* as well as the previous books in the *Tell Me What to Eat* series. She has her own Web site (recipedoctor.com) and contributes to several Web sites, including dietriot.com.